All the best —

Love,

Brad

The Big Red Schoolhouse

The Big Red Schoolhouse

FRED M. HECHINGER

Introduction by Paul Woodring

1959
Doubleday & Company, Inc., Garden City, New York

Library of Congress Catalog Card Number 59–6268
Copyright © 1959 by Fred M. Hechinger
All Rights Reserved
Printed in the United States of America
Designed by Diana Klemin
First Edition

To Grace

Acknowledgments

The author and Doubleday & Company are grateful to the following authors, magazines, newspapers, publishers, and others for permission to use material contained in this book:

Dr. George Z. Bereday and the New York *Herald Tribune* for an excerpt from the column by Terry Ferrer, "Month in Soviet Schools Sobers U. S. Educators," June 22, 1958. Reprinted by permission.

Patricia Blake and *The Reporter* for an excerpt from the article "Russia: The Scientific Elite," from the issue of November 14, 1957. Reprinted by permission.

Henry Brandon and the Sunday *Times* of London for an excerpt from "How Far Ahead Is Russia?" an interview with Isidor Rabi from the issue of November 7, 1957. Reprinted by permission.

George Counts and the McGraw-Hill Book Company, Inc., for a quotation by Alexis de Tocqueville from *The Challenge of Soviet Education*, by George Counts. Reprinted by permission of McGraw-Hill Book Company, Inc.

Nicholas DeWitt, for permission to reprint an excerpt from

Acknowledgments

Soviet Professional Manpower, published by National Science Foundation, Washington, D. C.

Max Lerner and the New York *Post* for an excerpt from the column "Four Fallacies on Our Schools," reprinted by permission of the New York *Post*, copyright 1958 New York *Post* Corporation.

Marc Raeff for material from the article "Report on Russia's Big Red Schoolhouse," June 22, 1958, the New York *Times*. Reprinted by permission of the author.

Rear Admiral H. G. Rickover for excerpts from the speech "Education in the Nuclear Age," delivered at New London, Connecticut, December 6, 1957. Reprinted by permission of E. P. Dutton & Company, Inc.

Society for Cultural Relations with U.S.S.R., London, for material from "The Overloaded Syllabus," in *Soviet Education Bulletin*, August 1957. Reprinted by permission.

Paul Woodring and McGraw-Hill for material from *A Fourth of a Nation*, reprinted by permission of McGraw-Hill Book Company, Inc.

Introduction

When the history of twentieth-century America eventually is written it will be recorded that the date of October 5, 1957, was a turning point in American education. Sputnik didn't do it all alone—the times were ripe for change. For ten years and more the schools had been undergoing a vigorous reassessment at the hands of the American people and their intellectual leaders. Writers on education had divided themselves into two opposing camps; those who viewed the schools with complacency and defended the status quo, and those who viewed with alarm and were sharply critical of the educational trends of our generation.

During this long period of critical examination, Fred Hechinger avoided being drawn into either of the extreme groups. As an educational reporter, analyst, writer, and editor, he reported the facts objectively, interpreted their underlying significance, commented vigorously, and analyzed the attacks and counterattacks. While free of bias he has never been neutral about the things that really matter. He has always stood for quality in education and has never been reluctant to dis-

9

tinguish between the significant and the trivial. Educators and parents alike, who have come to look to him for a calm and unbiased interpretation, and for a thoughtful probing into the significance of educational trends, will not be disappointed in the present book. Others, who have given less attention to educational problems, will discover that a book on education can be exciting, challenging, and highly readable.

Until late 1957, many American parents and other citizens had never really doubted that our schools were the best in the world. Even the decade of reassessment had raised doubts in the minds of only a minority. Because we had more schools, and bigger schools than other nations, and kept our children in them for a longer period of time, we assumed that our system of education must be better than that found in other lands. It was comforting to believe that the Russians substituted propaganda for liberal education, that their scientific and technical schools were inferior to ours, and that they had been able to develop an atomic bomb only by stealing our secrets.

With Sputnik I, our apathy was replaced by panic. One educator commented that many people who had never before given much attention to the problems of education "immediately went into orbit and started beeping." They demanded crash programs for the training of engineers and scientists. Some wanted a national system of education with standards set by a group of scholars. A few even talked of replacing our long commitment to universal education with a much more selective system.

Calmer voices pointed out that any changes made in the

schools today would not be reflected in our national leadership for at least twenty-five or thirty years and that the need was for long-range planning rather than for crash programs. It was emphasized that if we are to maintain our free institutions we must educate for freedom as well as for invention and production.

Some educators who were still contented with our schools continued to defend the status quo, but there were few to listen. The great majority of educators and other citizens alike were convinced that we must make some dramatic changes in all our schools from kindergarten through college. But before making these changes we needed more information about both our own schools and the schools of other lands from which we might be able to learn.

There was no end to information about our own schools, but because of the vast diversity of our educational establishment, with its local controls and uneven standards, the truth was difficult to assess. The truth about Russian schools was even more difficult to find. Only a few Americans had observed the Soviet schools at first hand, and those who had done so had been limited in their choice of what they might observe. A great deal of information might be gained by reading the individual reports of these people and by reading the many governmental publications and journal articles which had been published. But there was no single book, easily available to Americans, that brought the information together in a form useful to the general reader.

This volume is an answer to that need. Here is a clear and

vivid description of Russia's schools, a critical analysis of our own education, and an interpretation of the similarities and differences. Both systems are interpreted in terms of their historical antecedents and their underlying cultures.

American readers, unfamiliar with the complex history of Russian education, will find many surprises in this account. Even before the Revolution of 1917 there were some excellent schools in Russia with eight million children enrolled. The half million who went through the secondary schools provided a considerable nucleus of educated manpower. After the Revolution, in the 1920s, the U.S.S.R. went overboard in its acceptance of a view of education very similar to that called "Progressive Education" in the United States. "Learning by doing" and "the whole child" became the catch phrases, and "permissiveness" was carried, in Hechinger's words, "to its ultimate absurdity"—much farther than in the United States. The authority of the teacher "shriveled to nothing." Hechinger's explanation of why the communist leaders chose to let the schools go through the withering-away period of total permissiveness, is a brilliant hypothesis—perhaps the most important in the book, for it has implications for American education.

In the 1930s the party leaders liquidated the progressive leaders and the schools did an about face toward a more highly disciplined, subject-centered curriculum, with an emphasis on talent and high intellectual achievement. It is this newer education that is now seen by some as a threat to the United States.

Mr. Hechinger finds much to criticize in the Russian schools. Russian educational policy has vacillated wildly in an effort to conform to the ever-changing party line. There is too much rote learning and too little independent thinking. They have had no more success than we in adapting universal secondary education to the stubborn facts of individual differences in learning capacity.

But Russian students and teachers are much more highly motivated than ours. They work harder and have a clearer sense of purpose. Students get a thorough grounding in geography and in both ancient and modern history (although the history is somewhat warped to fit their own interpretation). They get an early introduction to mathematics and science. In one important respect their students are far less provincial than ours—Ivan is much more likely than Johnny to be able to converse in languages other than his own and to know the literature of other countries.

Although he avoids resorting to the scare technique, some of Mr. Hechinger's facts are frightening enough in themselves. Russia has glamorized the student, the teacher, the scholar, and the scientist, and rewards them well. The United States has scorned them as "eggheads" and offers them much less in both prestige and material rewards. The effect of this difference in roles on the quality and numbers of young people entering intellectual pursuits in the two nations can easily be predicted.

Russia's schools are an instrument of national policy. Our schools have been, in large part, molded by public demand in each individual community. The effective demands are not those of a clear majority but more often those of noisy minorities who want marching bands, public entertainment, and easy and practical courses which will keep children happy and off the street but which may have little long-range value. Many a discouraged superintendent of schools has said in effect, "all right, we shall teach anything you want us to teach," and the result has been chaos in the curriculum. We have confused the American dream of the pursuit of happiness with a pursuit of ease, comfort, and entertainment.

Even today it appears that the American people do not yet believe nearly as deeply in the importance of education as do the Russians. We believe in the symbols of education—we want our children to possess diplomas and degrees. We like the side shows of education, drum majorettes, and athletic contests—but the Russians believe in education itself and willingly make great sacrifices to get it.

Their view of what constitutes a good education is different from ours, and certainly they lack our great concept of the truly liberating education—that which frees the individual from the limitations of ignorance, prejudice and provincialism, and prepares him to make wise independent decisions as a citizen in a nation that allows freedom of choice. But some of our schools lack this great concept too.

The fact that Russia launched the first satellite was a blow to our national ego and carried an implied threat to our security. It didn't really change the problems of American education—the problems had been with us all along—but it did bring to us a greater awareness of the problems and created a climate of opinion in which action is possible.

We have long assumed that a free, public, universal education was essential to the good life as we conceive it. It is no less essential today. But now we have become aware that education—perhaps a better education than we have ever had—is essential to survival itself. The great danger is that, now the first period of panic is past, we shall again lapse into complacency before the necessary reforms in our schools have been achieved.

As an antidote to complacency and a signpost pointing to the road ahead, this is clearly the most important book on education of the post-Sputnik era.

Paul Woodring

Preface

Whenever education is discussed for consumption by a wide public, the temptation is to catch the reader's eye with the old barker's technique of the sensational "come-on." The motto seems to be: Expose, and conquer. If, for example, I could bluntly charge "Corruption in Kindergarten" or "White Slavery in Red Classrooms," the book would need no further introduction. Even a simple summary, such as "Soviet Schools Have Licked Us" or "U.S. Victory over Soviet Education," would do the trick without further explanation or apology.

But education and life are not that simple. Issues are not so clear-cut, and there are always more than two sides to every question. If the reader, worried about Russian or American education, wants an easy answer to the simple-minded question, "Who's ahead?" he will first have to tell me what aspects of the race interest him.

I don't believe that the gigantic struggle between two civilizations can be reported in the manner of a horse race. The comparison figures of the numbers of engineers and the relative salaries of scientists are only fragments of the vast

17

and fateful panorama. To become obsessed with the numbers game in the contest between the Soviet Union and the United States is a little like describing the battle of Gettysburg in terms of a quartermaster's list of equipment.

This book will thus sketch many aspects of the present line-up in this historic battle, in which the minds of millions of children can be considered the infantry. Their parents, their teachers, the schools and their administrators, and their governments are the "officers" weighing tactics, strategy, logistics. With this survey, the reader, I trust, will be in a far better position to choose a battle plan for the survival and improvement of his nation's schools.

To make that choice, the American citizen needs a balance of facts, somewhere midway between the panicky headlines and the soothing reassurance by many school superintendents and other educators that the American school system is the best ever. Some of the extreme crisis headlines are undoubtedly well intentioned. It has come to be an American habit to get money appropriations by scaring the daylights out of taxpayers, finance committees, and Congress. In raising funds to combat a disease, the donors are made to believe that death is just around the corner. Nothing could help a navy appropriation more than an alleged Red submarine off Ellis Island. So—why not scare the country into "doing something" about the schools?

I am skeptical about the scare technique, when applied to the schools, because I am afraid that reforms born of shock and panic may do serious and permanent harm to education.

I see grave danger in shock treatment, not because I think reforms are unnecessary, but rather because I think reforms, in order to turn the tide, must be far-reaching and long-range. A little emergency patching just won't do the trick. I want the reader to respond to facts rather than to fear, and some of the facts as I found them are fearful enough to cry out for action, without the benefit of sensationalism.

Education, I am fully aware, includes many things, people, and institutions other than the schools. There are the mass media, books, the colleges and universities. All of them are important. Each wields great educational power. Despite this, I have limited this comparative report to Russia's and America's elementary and secondary schools. The reason for this is that during those years of basic schooling the major impact is made on the generations of the future. Even the educational policies and power of the universities are, in the last analysis, at the mercy of the elementary and high schools. It is therefore in those schools that the battle of the mind will be lost or won.

Getting the facts on the American school is relatively easy: everything is above board and open for inspection. What makes it difficult is that there is no "system." The Russians have plenty of system, but few of the facts and statistics are open for inspection. It is therefore obvious that this book could not have been attempted without the use of a great wealth of research material, eyewitness reports, articles and books by dozens of able scholars.

To all of them goes my sincere acknowledgment. Their

writings are listed in the Appendix, both by way of giving due credit and of offering the reader firsthand sources for further study. But special thanks and admiration for their scholarly work go to Nicholas DeWitt, author of *Soviet Professional Manpower*, to Alexander G. Korol, author of *Soviet Education for Science and Technology*, and to the United States Department of Health, Education and Welfare for its publication, *Education in the U.S.S.R.*

My personal gratitude goes to my wife, Grace, without whose constant aid—from the drudgery of research to vital and imaginative ideas, criticism, and editing—this book could not have been written.

F.M.H.

Bridgeport, Connecticut.

Contents

Contents

22

1

Ivan or Johnny

Soon after the Russians launched the first Sputnik, an American broadcaster for the Columbia Broadcasting System described the education of Ivan, a typical teen-ager in Moscow, in a program straight from the Soviet capital. Ivan's schooling sounded hard and demanding. He learned plenty of mathematics. He read a good deal of both Russian and Western literature. He spoke English well, if not quite fluently. He had come to expect a pretty regular dose of homework. But, in all fairness, Ivan's school life was not all work. He had extracurricular fun, including amateur dramatics and sports.

CBS switched to a group of American high school students in Tennessee. What did they think of Ivan? The consensus was that too much work had undoubtedly made Ivan a dull boy. One of the American teen-age girls went so far as to state flatly that she would not enjoy a date with the young Russian because, she feared, they would have little to talk about. She considered all the many things Ivan was studying worse than a waste of time: she thought them boring. The other kids agreed. When asked what they thought was the important ingredient of a good high school education, they said the most valuable lesson they were learning was how to get along with other people.

On the surface the comparison was nothing short of devastating. The semiliterate ramblings of the teen-agers in Tennessee were aggravated by their parroting of semidigested social philosophies. Their condescending view of Ivan's learning made his education gain considerable stature by comparison. The fact that they were so self-assured about the virtue of their ignorance made their performance even more pathetic.

To those who had been shocked and alarmed by recent Soviet scientific and technical successes, the performance may have been shocking and alarming rather than pathetic. Of course, this was the effect the broadcast, like an avalanche of other radio reports, newspaper articles, and speeches, tried to achieve.

On the West Coast, a broadcaster caught a few American teen-age boys outside a high school and learned from them that, instead of mathematics, they were taking a course in co-ed cooking. Another volcano of popular indignation erupted. High school officials across the country quickly protested that only a small fraction of youngsters take such easy courses as substitutes for tougher education. All over the nation the debate over American versus Soviet education assumed priority over almost all other topics. It invaded polite afterdinner conversation and political speechmaking. Parents, already worried over the confusing (and often confused) question of the best kind of education for their children, became panicky when they heard statesmen, scientists, admirals, and university presidents argue over these questions before a national audience and in terms of national survival.

Many educators, afraid that they would wind up as the scapegoats of a nation which had suddenly grown unsure of its position of world leadership, counterattacked almost blindly. Their refrain: "Everything is fine. Just leave things as they are, but give us more money—and there will be nothing to fear." Sometimes their plea for the maintenance of the *status quo* was almost as panicky as the demand of the rest of the country for any kind of action—shock treatment and crash programs—at almost any price.

The two extremist views today are that we must either ignore the Russians and go along as though nothing had happened, or that we must abandon all earlier ideas and procedures and imitate what we think are the educational practices of the Russians.

This book has as its purpose the attempt to find, between the extremes, a road of reason. This need not be, and probably cannot be, a middle road, much as the middle road has come to be accepted as a political cure-all and the last word in safety and wisdom. There cannot be, in education, a middle road in the political sense, because education is not to be determined by compromise between two opposing views. In education there are not merely two sides to every question —nor even three or four or five. Education is rather like the surface of the diamond whose light and depth and splendor is determined by countless facets. Like the diamond, too, the process of education can be continuously refined and perfected. It never reaches perfection itself: there is always another diamond—more perfect. And there is always, even in the seemingly most perfect stone, a flaw, no matter how minute.

Today we know that there are serious flaws in the American education system—and in the product turned out by the American school. This makes us look with envy at the product of our currently most serious competitor, Russia. We are easily persuaded that its schools must be superior and its methods apparently marred by fewer flaws.

The temptation therefore is strong to imitate. "Catching up" is the favorite phrase of today. The trouble with both imitation and "catching up" is that, applied to education, they may lead to disaster; for education is a matter of evolution and adaptation. It cannot be determined in a vacuum; it must reflect the national character, the national problem, and, perhaps most of all, the national dream.

This does not mean that the discoveries of other nations and the competition among nations should not affect the process and the systems of education. They do and they should. But before we begin to change our system and our approach, and permit it to be influenced by the Russian experience, we must have a clear understanding of the facts. We must know what the Russians are doing and why. But we must also know more fully what we ourselves are doing and how well or how badly we are doing it.

Such knowledge is essential. It must be detached from both fear and wishful thinking. For too long we have been telling ourselves that America, the greatest nation on earth, had devised the greatest school system the world had ever seen. Thus our only problem was how to protect it from foreign or subversive influences. For several years, after World War II, this false sense of smugness led to the widespread belief that we needed only to keep a jealously watchful eye on our textbooks and our teachers so that the enemy could not infiltrate our schools with his treacherous heresies. This is an oversimplification of the kind generally arrived at by wishful thinking.

But fear leads to similar paralysis. Before World War II a small but eloquent minority was so afraid of the Fascist police states that they saw America's salvation largely in the acceptance of the Fascist superiority and in the imitation of the enemy's methods.

Ralph McGill, the great southern editor, put it somewhat differently. He warned that the American people must free themselves of what he called the rhythm between panic and apathy.

It would be foolish—and a fraud—to pretend that this book will offer the solution for America's school problems. The best it can try to do is make the search for the proper line of thought and action a little easier. In the process it can also point to the truth, so often purposely overlooked, that people and nations will continue to have to cope with all kinds of imperfections that no school, no matter how perfect, can eliminate. It is very easy for us, at each new report of juvenile delinquency and misbehavior, to shake our heads and blithely suggest that a little of that tough discipline of the Russian school could cure all that. It's easy, but it is also misleading. As recently as April 17, 1958, New York *Times* correspondent Max Frankel reported from Moscow that Soviet leaders were accusing Russian youths of being grafters, shirkers, and drunks and that they were "sitting around in big cities and whiling away the time in idleness." The most interesting sidelight to this story is that the Russians blame these shortcomings of their young people on "the propaganda and the culture of the West" while many Americans ask for imitation of the Russian education system as the road to salvation. The chances are that both are wrong, and this book ought to furnish the reasons why.

A nation's schools are not created in a vacuum. They are blessed and burdened with the background and the traditions of their people. While it is true that they are the die from which the generations of the future are cast, the die itself bears the marks of generations, even civilizations, that came before. A dictatorship, such as Soviet Russia, may try to wipe out the traditions and experiences of the past, while a democratic society works hard to preserve past greatness. But whether it is treated as friend or foe, asset or liability, the past is never neutral. It is as surely part of the present as heredity is the stamp put on the children by their parents.

This book, therefore, will take a close and unprejudiced look at the history of both the Russian and the American school. I will try to explain the heritage that shaped both the Russian and the American curricula. For years, perhaps decades, Russia and America, as the two great powers of the modern, mechanized world, will be engaged in a battle of giants. Even if the battle is to remain relatively peaceful (avoiding at least the ultimate doom of nuclear warfare), the contest will be both real and relentless. And if the future of the world was at one time determined on the playing fields of Eton, it is now being shaped in the public schools of the United States and the U.S.S.R.

This book, in the chapters ahead, will try to compare those schools dispassionately. It will not assume, as has been done so often in the past, that the "Made in the U.S.A." stamp is an automatic seal of superiority. It will look at the curriculum to find out what is being taught, hour for hour, and how well it is being learned.

There are many questions to be asked: How many children go to school and how much do they profit from it? What are the criteria by which students are judged and what are the uses to which their talents are put? How are the schools controlled and what is their immediate and long-range influence on their country?

But perhaps the most important twin questions, one so desperately dependent on the other, are:

Where will the Russians go from here? and

What should be the American plan for the future?

31

Chapter One

The pressure of the headlines and the panic of a battle fought largely in the darkness of ignorance have created the impression that the Russians have built a perfect school. This book will probe the measure of that perfection. It will try to highlight the Russians' achievements without overshadowing their problems and the weaknesses. It will, above all, attempt to predict the changes that are imminent in the Big Red Schoolhouse.

These predictions, based on current facts and rumblings, are important to how we shape the American future. Should we ape the Russian achievement? It would be tragic if such changes were to imitate a map that has already been found misleading by those who designed it.

A new map is already being drawn for the Soviet school. Where will it lead? A new map is undoubtedly needed for the American educational future. What should be its direction? After examining the history and the present facts of the Soviet and the American elementary and secondary schools, I want to provide, not a blueprint, but a signpost.

Russian Schools:
Czars, Purges
and
the New Soviet Man

Early in 1956, I spent the better part of two weeks showing Mme. Ludmila Dubrovina, the Deputy Minister of Education for the Russian Soviet Federated Socialist Republic, the ins and outs of American education as represented by the schools of New York City and its suburbs. I had often heard American critics of the present school system refer to modern or progressive education as Communist- or Soviet-inspired. Although I knew enough about the background and meaning of progressive education to realize that these accusations were completely false, I also recalled that the Soviet Union had, in fact, embraced the progressive method and idea for quite a number of years following the Bolshevik revolution of 1917.

With this in mind, I asked Mme. Dubrovina why the progressive trend had been abandoned. "Because we found it to be incorrect," was her simple reply.

"Incorrect" is an important word to keep in mind in any discussion of Soviet education. It crops up dozens of times in almost every official directive and governmental critique.

35

There are only two alternatives in the orthodox Soviet mind—to be "correct" or "incorrect." To follow an incorrect line means to be working in opposition to the State. Moreover, the "correct" line is determined, not as a fixed and permanent guidepost, but as the current path, always subject to change and, not infrequently, to complete reversal.

I asked Mme. Dubrovina whether there were not, among the thousands of Soviet teachers, some who were not convinced that the modern or progressive "line" had been totally false. Would such teachers still be able to experiment with their educational ideas and theories?

"But there are no such teachers," she replied, not so much in stubborn opposition to the thoughts my question implied as with the impatience a mother might show toward the foolish question of an ignorant child. "They have been shown that their way was incorrect," she said. "Why should they persist, now that they have been shown the correct way?"

I continued: "But assume that some teachers would like to go on with their experimentation."

"They would only be wasting their pupils' time," Mme. Dubrovina said, and she considered the subject closed. Shortly after she returned to the Soviet Union, Mme. Dubrovina was placed in charge of the rewriting of Russian textbooks. This was soon after the downgrading of Joseph Stalin and the denunciation of the "cult of personality" as a governmental ideological line. In her own terminology, she would undoubtedly consider her new task that of replacing "incorrect" books (which she had until that moment helped to provide for all Soviet youngsters) with "correct" editions.

Whatever else may be said about this kind of educational system, it is adaptable. An order by the Supreme Soviet can, at any time, demand a new set of goals—even goals directly opposite to the earlier ones. The entire machine can be put in reverse or moved forward in a different direction. This is not, let's face it, a totally unattractive idea to some industrialists who would like to achieve exactly that kind of flexibility in their production lines. Efficiency is the speed with which the plant can be retooled to respond to a change in consumer demand. There is no question that the apparent ability of the Soviet education system to respond to the immediate demand of a science-minded and rocket-competitive world has become the envy of many Americans.

How has this system evolved? What were the historic facts behind Mme. Dubrovina's firm conviction that whatever changes have taken place signified simply the transition from "incorrect" to "correct" practice?

Pre-Revolution schools in Russia reflected clearly the feudal culture of the Czarist period. The vast nation relied on the gigantic reservoir of untutored peasants, at best literate enough to measure the seed, weigh the harvest, and market the produce. The literate elite went through the same process of education as did the elite of Central Europe—in the German gymnasium or in the French *lycée*. That this elite was highly literate, cultured, and educated in the truest sense of the word is obvious to anyone who has read Russian literature.

37

It reflects a deep sense of history and the kind of understanding of the human struggle that can only flow from a broad and sensitive liberal education. If the schools limited their offerings to a small minority, they followed nevertheless the established practice of Western society of their day. Perhaps they based their selection even more exclusively on noble birth and occasional corruption than did their German and French counterparts. If so, they again reflected merely the values of the society in which they functioned and whose demands they served. Those were, after all, the times when even Germany and France, despite the beginning rumblings and demands of industrialization, sent only fewer than 5 per cent of their population through the high schools. It was only natural that Russia, still plodding along as a sleepy agricultural giant, made the pipeline toward academic achievement even thinner. The rulers were satisfied with a tiny trickle of educated men and women. Don't forget that even as recently as the 1940s some economists, even in the United States, were warning against an "educated proletariat." Under the circumstances it was hardly surprising that societies like Czarist Russia looked on advanced education—and high school education then was considered advanced—as a luxury to be reserved for the upper classes and the professions.

But it would be a serious error—an error that is being promoted by Soviet propagandists today—to assume that pre-Revolution Russia did not have a system of truly first-rate education. Its schools were limited to the aristocracy and the landed gentry, but they were good schools and good universities. They were built after the model of the best Central European schools, mainly the German ones, and their influence on Russian life, at least among the "social elite," was profound.

Throughout the last century of Czarist rule, there were actually several attempts to broaden the basis of education and to admit the children of the lower classes. In the main, those attempts were unsuccessful, partly because of the overwhelming administrative inefficiency of this giant country. But more compelling was the fear of the rulers that education would, unless properly controlled by them, lead to their own downfall.

This was an understandable fear. Practically all the liberal and revolutionary movements in Europe had been led by the educated youth, especially of the universities. While modern dictatorships, as documented by the Soviets, find it quite possible (though not necessarily easy) to control education and exploit it for their own benefit, the autocratic rulers of the past thought it easier to control the masses by not giving them access to the power that comes from knowledge. In the first half of the nineteenth century, for instance, Count S. S. Uvarov, Minister of Education under Czar Nicholas I, demanded that the Russian schools dedicate themselves to "the truly Russian conservative principles of orthodoxy, autocracy and nationalism." When apparently even this limited system of education threatened to lead to greater portions of free thoughts and personal independence, he warned that education and the greater popular demand for it "should not be suffered to disturb in any way the existing class system, by awakening in youthful minds the impulse to acquire unnecessary knowledge, which cannot be applied in practice." Without getting too far ahead of our story, this insistence on "practical application" of education became one of the anchors of Soviet education and—to go a step further—is still hotly advocated by a considerable body of opinion in America.

But even the most autocratic rulers of Czarist Russia sensed that better schooling was essential to the future of Russia. The only defense, then, and the only assurance that they would not see their absolute power usurped by educated masses was to keep the masses away from all but the most basic education. In 1887 the Russian Minister of Education told the secondary schools, which were based on the German gymnasium, that they were under no circumstances to admit "the children of coachmen, lackeys, cooks, washerwomen, small tradesmen, and their kind."

Despite these precautions, the growth of education—much of it of high caliber in direct contradiction to the edicts of the politicians—led to a greater demand for liberty. There were the beginnings of serious rumblings, of student strikes and violent demonstrations as early as the mid-nineteenth century.

For a time, mounted police and Czarist troops were able to provide a sufficiently convincing reply. But underneath the apparently successful repression was the more vexing conflict. The rulers themselves were plagued by the inevitable and nagging question of how to retain their power among an educated populace. And when they answered to themselves that they would not be able to do so, they were haunted by the equally fundamental question of how Russia would ever turn herself into a modern, Western nation without a modern network of schools. The conflict was never resolved. But the orthodoxy of the autocrats seems to have weakened enough for new streams of education—which were about to become dominant in some parts of Central Europe and which, a little later, played a vital part in the American development—to influence Russia. Making the school a place where the child had fun and where the teacher became a friend and adviser rather than a figure of authority, even of terror, was the theme of some of the leading Russian theorists in the last part of the nineteenth century.

When the revolution snipped off the historic cords that had held Russian history, orthodoxy, and reluctant progress together, the Bolsheviks were presented, not only with a majority of illiterates (a statistic the Communists enjoy repeating), but also with a better network of schools than is generally known. Almost 8,000,000 Russians were enrolled in well over 106,000 schools. But even more important, more than half a million students were attending high schools of European character and quality. This is not a high number by today's standards, but its a considerable nucleus of educated manpower for a peasant country prior to its industrial revolution.

The Bolshevik Revolution swept away all the foundations of Russian society as it had been known under the Czars.

When the smoke of battle cleared and the new regime established itself on the new foundations of Marxist slogans and dialectics, the "official" view on education matched that of the State. The politicians predicted that the State, after a transition period, would wither away. The educators forecast a similar withering away of the school.

It is entirely possible that some of the sloganeers of those days actually believed their predictions, much as the original leaders of the French Revolution actually believed in absolute freedom and the followers of Thoreau believed in the possibility of an ideal State of self-ordered anarchy without evil and without taxation. But while the politicians kept the withered-away State carefully stored in the mothballs of an indefinite future, the educators rushed headlong into the first phase of their own prediction.

On the surface they had a good case on their side. The schools of the exclusive and strongly class-conscious societies, such as those of Imperial Germany and Czarist Russia, were not only discriminatory in their selection—that sin could have been corrected by nothing more serious than a new admissions policy—but they had also grown stale, unimaginative, autocratic, and oblivious of the differences in the minds of children.

Historically the time was ripe for a change. In Germany and Switzerland the influence of Pestalozzi and his followers had begun to make deep inroads into the traditional school, replacing the domineering attitude of a teacher-dictator with the understanding of a guiding friend. This new approach,

with its mixture of academic learning, handicraft, and farm-
ing, had breathed new life into musty and dusty minds of the
old pedant pedagogues for whom learning was an exerise in
mental gymnastics rather than a human experience. The new
philosophy spoke of the three Hs: Head, Heart, and Hand.

In the United States, John Dewey and his disciples had
begun to spread the gospel of "learning by doing" and of
the school's duty to be concerned, not with the child's mind
alone, but with the education of "the whole child." Everywhere the teacher was dethroned from his physical superiority on a raised podium. The lecture became the mark of
educational reaction. The seminar and work-study project
were the new-found road to the emancipation of the pupil.

These revolutionary movements were not hatched, as it
is frequently hinted today, in some conspiratorial back rooms
of Columbia Teachers College. They were not divorced from
the general trends and currents of the time. On the contrary,
they followed naturally the new influence of psychology and
the popularization of the teachings of Freud, Adler, and
Jung. These innovations reflected, too, the political awakening by great masses of people who demanded removal of the
dam that kept the majority of a nation's children out of the
channels of high school and college education. They followed
the sweeping political and ideological currents originally set
in motion by the French Revolution and by the more gentle
but no less determined popular voices of a Thomas Jefferson
and a Thomas Paine. After a century, equality had become
the password in everyday politics. The "self-evident" truth

that all men were created equal inevitably required that all children be given equal opportunities to climb the educational ladder. As new interpretations were put to the political and social philosophy of equality, careless thinkers and opportunistic disciples interpreted the "equality" to mean that there should be no distinction between men and women of different talents and abilities. Give the child complete freedom to grow, this comfortable doctrine held, and he will grow to his full height. From the autocratic teacher who rewarded the pupil who could memorize most completely the stale and dogmatic lesson that was forced on his mind, the pendulum swung to the extreme of unguided "self-expression" of the untutored child.

It was at this point, in the early 1920s, that the Russian Revolution and its educators jumped on the careening bandwagon of total permissiveness. Their theory of the withering away of the school was already being applied. The teacher had been demoted and, in the extreme instances of a misinterpreted progressive school, condemned to impotence. At best, he was permitted to remain at the rear of the class and to offer an opinion, if asked. The teacher's authority had shriveled to nothing.

In most Western or American schools the extremists were never permitted to carry this experiment to its ultimate absurdity. There were enough good and strong teachers around to resist the charlatans. There were the normal safeguards of a diversified system, not subject to the orders or the control of any central authority. There were the strong brakes, applied by the deans of admissions of the leading universities. These men had the strength and the prestige to demand that applicants be taught what continued to be considered the basic requirements for higher education.

None of those safeguards, however, existed in Russia. On the contrary, the safeguards and the conservative voices were attacked as the tools of reaction and the devil's own temptation to lead the revolution into "incorrect" paths.

The Russians went all the way. They raised the new banner of "polytechnic" education which, at that stage of Soviet development, meant "learning by doing" and learning only the things which could at once be translated into practical and manual results. Schools were run by student-elected committees. Even elementary school pupils had a voice equal to their teachers. The popular slogan was that the school was to become "the adjunct to the factory." Book learning was discredited. Communist youth leaders—still in their adolescent years—not only spied on the teachers but could countermand their orders and free pupils from classroom work. Examinations and graded efforts were labeled the marks of bourgeois reaction and were abolished. Homework was prohibited.

This was the phase in which foggy visionaries were permitted to let their chaotic social theories run riot while, in the background, the political rivals fought for the consolidation of revolutionary power. It was the period of free love and of an army without ranks. It was the time when even Russian diplomats could not wear neckties lest they be considered bourgeois traitors.

The Russian school at this point turned into a tragic parody of freedom.

The orgy of "freedom" came to a sudden end in the thirties. To the outside world this appalling phase in Soviet development was symbolized by mass trials and murderous purges, by the consolidation of Stalin's supreme power and the abject confessions and self-accusations of his enemies. Far from having withered away, the State reasserted a despotic power more total than the imperial rule of the Czars. In the process of "liquidation" of the old spokesmen and leaders, the heads of the progressive education advocates rolled first. The pendulum had taken another swing back to the opposite extreme. The armed forces were again organized along lines of command that resembled the Prussian staff system. Puritanism routed free love. The traditonal school, built around the authority of the teacher, was brought back with a vengeance. Orders and directives rained down from the Supreme Soviet on the heads of local educators. The powers of the Ministries of Education of each of the sixteen Soviet Republics were clearly and strongly established.

From a practical point of view of national development this next step was a natural and extremely important one. The watchword of the future was industrialization, and the goals were set without regard for human discomfort and suffering. Manpower was the tool which alone could promise attainment of the goal, and the school had to be the die which was to cast the human material into the required mold. Stalin spoke of the schools as the fortress and the arsenal with which the battle of industrialization and world domination had to be won.

Under normal circumstances and in a country undergoing the evolutionary changes of history, the tremendous contrasts—from chaotic progressive schools to the autocratic school that resembled in organization, if not in content, the Czarist school of pre-Revolution days—might have been explained away by the demands of rapid industrialization. But in the Soviet case this would be a misleading oversimplification. It must be remembered, at every step of the growth and progress of the Soviet school, that the Soviet view of education is a simple and uncomplicated one: the school must serve the goals set for the State by the Communist regime.

There is nothing evolutionary in this kind of progress. The school is simply adjusted, at each stage of Soviet development, to the service of the particular scene in the drama. The play itself has been written and approved, but the setting for each act is different and the roles in it demand new qualities of its actors. It is the task of the school to produce the actors.

This should not imply that the school, in other countries, including the United States, is not expected and required to serve the aims of its civilization and the purposes of the society which pays for the schools. But those aims and purposes themselves are only vaguely defined. The schools, therefore, are only vaguely directed toward those aims. True, they are expected to instill certain fundamental loyalties and a basic understanding of the virtues that have been traditionally accepted as the moral framework of Western thought and action. True also, the schools are expected to furnish the labor force—unskilled, skilled, white-collar, intellectual, and managerial—which must keep society vital and prosperous. But as a free civilization itself is slowly evolutionary, so are its schools.

The Russian story was quite different. It would be relatively easy to explain the "return" to autocratic, subject-centered education in the thirties as the self-explanatory answer to the demands of industrialization. But what kind of plausible explanation could be offered for the permissive period of chaos—the interlude of the withering away of the school, of the powerful student councils, and of the impotent teachers?

A morbidly fascinating explanation is that the educators who were in charge of "progressive" education in the 1920s had no idea why their masters, the politicians, not only let them go ahead but actually encouraged them. They were so completely unaware of the purpose for which they were being "used" and they were so dedicated to their great experiment that the majority of them blundered blindly into the great purges of the thirties which wiped out the phase of Soviet history with which they had been linked.

The leaders of the progressive, liberal era—among them Lenin's widow, N. K. Krupskaia, and S. T. Shatsky, a leading disciple of the American John Dewey—were thought by their Western and American colleagues to be truly devoted and capable exponents of the new approach to learning. Paul Blonsky, who followed closely the works of Western child psychologists and of the American experimenters with intelligence and aptitude testing, introduced pedagogy into the Soviet curriculum of teacher training. In 1936—on the eve of the great purges—his contribution was termed a perversion of science. Blonsky was wiped out, along with his theories.

Was the "experiment" that dominated the Soviet school for more than a decade merely a mistake? Is it true, as Mme. Dubrovina told me, that the methods of the early Soviet school were simply found "incorrect" and voluntarily abandoned? How voluntary the changes were is documented by the "disappearance" of all the education leaders who had been responsible for the "experiment." Who, then, had found the "old" methods incorrect—and why?

The answer is so cynical as to be almost incomprehensible to the free mind, to those who have always viewed education with Western eyes and measured it with the yardstick of Judeo-Christian civilization. But there is little doubt that the farce of the "withering away of the school" was played out consciously and purposely in order to eliminate the power of the old school and undermine the domination of the pre-Revolution intellectuals.

The Bolsheviks knew that the older teachers could not be trusted to become their servants. Even the Communist or pro-Communist teachers—and considering the nature of Czarist repression many teachers were attracted by the promise of the Revolution—had been educated as thinking men and women, guided by civilized ideals.

The Bolsheviks wanted the revolution to be total, and they were ready to achieve their ends, step by step, no matter how much time and planning and human sacrifice it would take.

The Bolsheviks knew that they would have to build a new school. They did not yet know or care what the content of the Soviet school would be ten or twenty years later, but it would have to be new in terms of the teachers and administrators who would run the schools.

To achieve this, the Bolsheviks decided they would first have to destroy the old school. They gave it the tools—for its own self-destruction. To this extent, the slogan of the withering away of the school—the old school—was not a complete lie.

Not only did the school become so "child-centered" that the teacher's role receded, but the teacher's powers were actually limited by new laws. The student government, moreover, became a powerful political weapon, with the youngsters encouraged to report on their elders, both teachers and parents. Lenin ordered the school to be more concerned with socially useful works—the extermination of cockroaches in slum tenements or the harvesting of potatoes on the farms or the building of roads in the villages. The curriculum of learning was steadily diluted. "The school that does" was to replace "the school that talks." The brash and self-important young leaders of the Young Pioneers could barge into the classroom and call students out for anything at all, from parades to "socially useful" community projects. The teacher had no voice in the matter. Since examinations and grades had been abolished, he could not even retaliate by demanding a minimum fare of learning and knowledge.

If anybody doubted that this was an effective way of "abolishing" the power and influence of the school and of the teaching profession, he was given additional proof several years later, in the thirties, when Hitler's National-Socialist school authorities followed almost exactly the same path. Here, too, the child—under the regimented auspices of the Hitler Youth organization—was given supreme powers. Uniformed adolescents were permitted to overrule and terrorize the teacher. Children were urged to inform on the activities of their parents and teachers. Had the Nazi regime outlived the span of time required to train a new set of teachers, the Nazi school would undoubtedly have become as strong a pillar of the dictatorship as the Soviet school came to be, once its supreme authority was re-established.

By 1928 the old Czarist school had been buried, with the blessings of the shrewd politicians and of the unsuspecting "progressive" educators. Then, Stalin's orders for rapid industrialization called for a different kind of school—a school which would train, at maximum speed, the human cogs in the machinery of new progress. The old "projects" were no longer of any use. Who cared about "socially useful work" or the extermination of cockroaches? The only socially useful work was to provide the manpower needed for industry.

The new purpose—supreme and single-minded—was "knowledge." The reversal was complete. While "book knowledge" and traditional teaching of subject matter had been ridiculed in the "unified labor school" of the twenties, it now was introduced as the central purpose of the school.

It is, of course, not unusual for educational theories to undergo important changes in any society. But the changes normally are evolutionary and slow, with the different streams of thought and method competing with each other and, not infrequently, blending into a new and different pattern. How slow these changes are in a free society, where forces and counterforces are constantly at work, can be seen from the American saying that to change the curriculum is like moving a cemetery.

By contrast, the Soviet change was carried out overnight. An official text of Soviet pedagogy of the first phase, edited by I. A. Kairov, said bluntly: "Revolutionary youth, standing on the side of Soviet power, played a large role in demolishing the old and creating the new Soviet school."

A new and "pure" generation of teachers was now available, even if many of them were badly educated. The "experimental" epoch was ordered closed. The school was given a new mandate: instead of "socially useful work" it was to provide the semiskilled, skilled, and highly skilled manpower needed for the glories of industrialization. The school was now to be an all-powerful conveyer belt, and the commodity to be assembled in it was to be trained humanity.

As always, in any shift of Soviet policy, the old terms were retained but given new meaning—often diametrically opposed to the old concepts. For instance, the new Soviet school was ordered to continue to offer "polytechnical education." But while the term earlier had been interpreted to mean "learning by doing," without regard for the "traditional" or "bourgeois" or even "counterrevolutionary" subject matter, the orders now were reversed. "Every attempt," said a 1931 directive of the party's Central Committee, "to separate the polytechnization of the school from a systematic and firm mastery of the sciences, and of physics, chemistry, and mathematics in particular, constitutes the most flagrant perversion of the ideas of the polytechnical school."

If the school of the twenties had prided itself in its informality and progressive shapelessness, the new school was to be strictly organized, with a rigid outline of studies to be demanded of all students—studies which were to be required without variation throughout the entire ten-year stretch of public education.

The "project method" was virtually outlawed. The Young Pioneers were ordered to keep their hands off the schools. The teachers, after all, could now be trusted to be servants of the state; they no longer needed to be humiliated or spied upon. A directive of 1932 demanded "the liquidation of the perversions of the laboratory-brigade approach," that "progressive" combination of field trips and "socially useful" forced labor.

If anyone had any doubt about the direction in which the "new" Soviet school was heading, he needed only to read this 1932 directive: "The chief form of the organization of instruction in the primary and secondary school must be the recitation with a given group of pupils following a strict schedule of studies. Under the leadership of the teacher this form must include group, brigade and individual work of each pupil."

Even the student government's purposes were reversed. Instead of making the student leaders the virtual bosses of the school, as they had been during the twenties, the only responsibility that was entrusted to them now was to push their fellow students into harder work and greater devotion to their studies. Instead of acting as whips to keep the teachers in line, they now were assistants to the teachers in enforcing strict student discipline.

But if all this sounds like a complete turnabout there was one purpose that remained the same: the use of the school to create the new Soviet man. The only thing that really had changed was the demands that were to be made on that man.

The growing "cult of personality"—as the dialectical post-Stalin dictionary terms it—even began to have its influence on the schools. For while the school of the twenties, almost constantly engaged in "socially useful work," never singled out the individual and considered acceptable only the competition between schools and classes, the trend now was toward intense personal competition. Students were singled out for achievement. Their grades, once more expressed in the old, traditional European progression from 5 (outstanding) to 1 (failing), were posted on school bulletin boards. Pictures of the best students were given publicity to inspire others to harder work. This is not surprising: an industrialized, technological society must rely heavily on able leaders and managers—and the collective approach rarely, if ever, yields leadership with real initiative and imagination.

But while all the upheaval may create the impression of great confusion, these startling and vital statistics must be remembered: before World War I the total number of pupils in Russian elementary and secondary schools was 8,000,000. By 1928, the end of the Soviets' "permissive" first phase, it had increased to 12,000,000. Before Russia's involvement in World War II—just twelve years later—the number had almost tripled to 35,000,000, and although the war brought a decline to about 30,000,000 by 1955, the tide has again begun to rise.

A great World War temporarily stopped Russia's march toward the goal Stalin set. But with Western support, the Soviet colossus withstood the onslaught and survived the terrible bloodletting. It continued along the road its leaders had mapped out. The schools were ordered to fulfill their quotas, much in the way in which the collective farms and the workers were commanded to deliver the harvest and the goods.

Whatever their ways and methods were (and they will be

explained in detail later), they seem to have succeeded in giving Russia the men and women who have turned the sleeping peasant giant into a roaring industrial superman. When the Soviets first caught up with American production of atomic and hydrogen weapons and, a little later, outdistanced the United States in the first bid for the conquest of outer space, the immediate and understandable reaction was that the Russian school had surpassed its American rival.

Whether this conclusion is true or false, it is inevitable that the American school will be asked to assume great responsibility for America's future in the struggle for world leadership. Will the American school be able to respond to the demands that are sure to be made? Before any answer can be attempted, let's see where the American school stands today—and how it got to be what it is.

3

The American Dream:
Quantity and Quality

The philosophy of education in the American colonies, under the British rule, was surprisingly similar to the philosophy that ruled the schools in Czarist Russia. The difference was one of degree. In Russia the limitations and restrictions were dictated by an absolute monarchy. In British terms the limitations and restrictions were dictated by an aristocracy with some public conscience working with a sometimes benevolent group of merchants. The similarity was, first, that in each case the educational emphasis was on "restrictions and limitations." It was second in the sources and origins of education. The tradition of German-French scholarship dominated both the Russian Czarist and the colonial American school, although the latter was modified by less pedantic British traditions.

To talk about universal education at that stage of history would have been absurd—no less so than to talk about public schools for the slaves in that first democracy in history, Athens. The very well-to-do American colonists were able to hire tutors for their children. For the remainder of the nobility and gentry, including those who planned to serve the church, there were church schools and Latin schools, based on the European curriculum and aimed at the education of ministers or gentlemen. Perhaps the best clue to the purpose of American colonial education is in the fact that Harvard University started with a single aim—still engraved in stone over the Harvard Yard—to avoid leaving "an illiterate Ministry to the Churches."

It was only slowly that the so-called charity schools were established to augment the few church schools. The merchants needed helpers with some slight skills. In addition, the poverty, filth, sickness, and drunkenness born of ignorance made a semblance of basic schooling seem increasingly desirable in the eyes of the colonial fathers.

To talk of American education before the American revolution is a contradiction in terms. It assumes that there could have been schooling with modern American aims and purposes before there had been created a society which set itself aims and purposes that were deliberately American. Whether in a democracy or in a complete police state, education always serves the society of which it is part. The fact that the colonies were in a part of the world known as America did not make them part of an American society any more than the schools of India in the pre-Commonwealth, colonial days served Indian society.

Thus the modern problems of the American school began with the American Revolution and with American independence. Only then did an American society first start to exist.

One of the immediate issues that the new society had to face was the kind of schools it wanted and was willing to support.

American society began to establish its own standards and aims in the atmosphere of the coming of the industrial age and of the gradual conquest of a vast continent.

Even then, it was not at all certain what direction America would choose. There were strong forces of aristocratic republicanism, normally perhaps a contradiction in terms but not at all a contradiction in the eyes of the disciples of Alexander Hamilton. On the other hand, the doctrines of Jeffersonian democracy, with their basic trust in the God-given power of the people, called for an increasingly educated people.

Other currents and countercurrents were at work. The farm interests were often quite different from the interests of the merchants. As the cities grew, the gulf between rural and urban living and thinking widened. To the early pioneers, who considered the hands that tilled the soil and grew the corn to be the fundamental strength of the nation, a country which can today look forward to an economy in which fewer than 5 per cent of the population can provide more than enough home-grown food would be unbelievable.

It would not have occurred to the pioneers and to the fathers of the nation, therefore, to call for a public school system of the kind we now consider part and parcel of American democracy. They wanted more and more men and women who mastered the skills needed in the fields and the workshops. They demanded, if they were believers in the words of the gospel, that the growing generations could understand and read the Bible. They considered, if they were lords of the manor, especially in the plantation country of the South, that it was the right of the gentlemen of the upper classes to be educated as gentlemen. They urged, if they believed in the dignity of all men, that poverty, disease, and ignorance among the lower classes be reduced, at least through the expansion of the charity schools which provided a skeleton of basic schooling.

There may not have been any agreement on the kind of schools America was to have; but each of these forces, with its own interests and doctrines, knew that schools had to be provided.

In the beginning there was little, if any, thought of free and universal public education. In fact, there continued a good deal of the sentiment that had prevailed among the upper classes in Czarist Russia. Remember the warning, issued in 1887 to Russia's secondary schools by the Minister of Education: to keep out "the children of coachmen, lackeys, cooks, washerwomen, small tradesmen, and their kind." In the 1830s the *National Gazette* in Philadelphia said bluntly: "The peasant must labor during those hours of the day which his wealthy neighbor can give to the abstract culture of his mind; otherwise the earth would not yield enough for the subsistence of all: the mechanic cannot abandon the operation of his trade, for general studies; if he should, most of the conveniences of life and objects of exchange would be wanting; languor, decay, poverty, and discontent would soon be visible among all classes."

Only a little more than 100 years have passed since this ideological statement of the difference between the laboring and the leisure classes. Yet, the short span of a century has led to the modern view that universal education will guarantee, among other things, a higher standard of living and better earnings. Within those 100 years, a system of education was created—not in a vacuum, but with a clear, though not always conscious, vision of the aims and purposes of society it was to serve.

There had been a good deal of argument in the early days of the republic whether or not there should be a national organization of education. All the European experience, which did, after all, provide the only available guide, pointed in that direction. But a national system, obviously, would have to be supported by taxation. It also meant that here would be another way of strengthening the powers of the central government, of giving the govenment an important additional function.

There was strong support for such a plan. The Jeffersonians and all the other proponents of a strong popular democracy insisted that giving great new powers to the people would be a dangerous adventure unless the people could be educated and given a chance to comprehend the issues that were to face them. A representative popular government, they knew could only be prevented from turning into chaotic mob rule if the people's representatives were to be educated men. Those who subscribed to the "self-evident" truth that "all men are created equal" could not possibly subscribe at the same time to either a system of education that kept out "cooks and coachmen" or to a school that gave preference to members of the leisure class. Jefferson said simply: "We hope to avail the state of those talents which nature has sown as liberally among the poor as the rich but which perish without use if not sought for and cultivated." Society, as these men saw it, believed strongly in the basic goodness and the inherent value of all men; thus all men should be given the benefits of education which would be paid for by the labor of all men: taxation.

There was the rub. The independent farmers, the urban merchants, and the southern slaveowners, all took a decidedly dim view of paying for the education of another man's children. Public education, on a national and publicly financed scale, was abandoned. It was out of this decisive abandonment, coupled with a real desire of a great many people to do something about the schooling of the children, that the strange compromise of leaving education to local jurisdiction first arose.

This is important to keep in mind. The general opinion today is that "local control" was originated as an ideal and an ideology, to prevent federal control. This is not historically true. While a minority actually did try to limit the powers of the federal government, the more general opposition to a national school drew its strength from a simple reluctance to pay taxes. Thus they took an amorphous approach that grew into 100,000 separate school districts by 1930. (Only the 1950s began to see some consolidation, with about 50,000 districts today.)

In the last prepublic school stage around the middle of the nineteenth century, the independent academies became the backbone of American education. The first independent academy had been proposed by Benjamin Franklin in 1749. Since these were established primarily by the ruling group of merchant capitalists, they moved swiftly away from the classical Latin-dominated traditions of the church schools and started to stress the more "practical" subjects. The advent of Darwinian thought in 1859 helped inject science into the curriculum. The academies followed the pattern of the "reformed" secondary schools of Germany and the "public schools" of England. They tried to find a compromise in which some of the traditional education of gentlemen could be merged with the requirements of modern life in an environment of industrial growth. It was out of industrialization— combined with the Jeffersonian idea of an educated populace—that the public schools first emerged during the second half of the nineteenth century. With the rise of the labor movement—led in its beginning by men such as Samuel Gompers, who were social reformers as much as they were trade unionists—came clear-cut demands that all children, regardless of class or wealth, be given an equal educational opportunity. Just as the Czars in the old Russian society (or the gentry in early American days) had been aware of the power of education if retained as a monopoly privilege in their hands, so the leaders of the labor movement knew that the promise of true equality, with all the prestige and power needed by an "equal" block within the pattern of society, could not be achieved without an educated rank and file.

The labor leaders fought for the privilege of universal public education during the second half of the nineteenth century. The spokesmen of social reform pleaded and persuaded. In much the same vein as education leaders today try to persuade industrialists to contribute to the support of the colleges and universities in order to strengthen the economy, Horace Mann, the symbol of the rising public education system, told the merchant opposition that "education has a market value." He warned that "in a Republic, ignorance is a Crime." In the end, though they had completely different aims in mind, the industrialists and the workers joined forces and helped to create the public schools.

The form of American education, if not its goals, moved along pretty much in the groove of the European tradition until the early part of the twentieth century. By that time the first battle had been won. The great majority of parents had been persuaded that school was a privilege they ought not to withhold from their children. Once the wealthier and socially more "respectable" neighbor had advanced on the education ladder, the rest of the neighborhood wanted to follow. Besides, most of the immigrants came from countries where the prestige of the teacher and of the educated man or woman was high. There was comparatively little need to "sell" education to mothers. Some of the fathers, rugged "self-made men," scoffed at book learning and considered school, certainly high school, "sissy stuff." But social pressures and the growing influence of women—another American phenomenon—easily won the day for the universal school. By 1900 almost 700,000 were enrolled in high schools. When, in addition, the demand of industry for technically versed manpower made high school education a necessity rather than a luxury, there was no longer any question about the triumph of mass education.

The great break in the traditional pattern of American education came between 1900 and 1920, almost at the same time as the establishment of the first post-Revolution school system in Russia. It was not a sudden break. The change was bound to come, because an old system of learning and teaching had been superimposed on completely new conditions. Where the school, in the past, had been consciously and proudly dealing with the training and refinement of the minds of a selected group, the mass school of America set out to serve the minds of all people. The students presented a range of talents and limitations as wide as the range of the population itself.

To prove the premises both right and workable, America had to create a new and different school. It was based on the pragmatic philosophy of doing what was needed and what was workable rather than on the old classical philosophy that education was fixed and predetermined and that it was up to the pupil to prove that he could "take it."

The American school, geared to the new ideal of mass

education, had to look for new ways. Fortunately, it was at this turn in educational history that new currents began to flow, not only in the United States, but also in Europe. The key word to the new approach was "psychology." Until the last quarter of the nineteenth century, psychology had been merely a subdivision of philosophy. By 1900 it had become what it is today: a science. Man's behavior now was no longer interpreted in terms of different philosophical views of mankind and its relationship to the world. Man's behavior became an important factor in a child's education—a factor to be considered in his reactions, in methods of teaching, in the type of subject matter presented to him at certain stages of his development. These discoveries led to a change in the very organization of the American public school. While the traditional pattern had been that of eight years of elementary and four years of high school (as compared with the European tradition of four years of elementary and eight or nine years of secondary school), the child psychologists called for a different kind of subdivision. They argued that between the first few grades and the last years of high school these are the distinct and often difficult stages of adolescence. The three categories, they warned, should be kept apart, if possible in separate buildings.

Thus, between 1900 and the twenties, a great many school districts (though not all of them) were converted from the so-called 8–4 plan to the 6–3–3 system: six years of elementary school; three years of "adolescent" junior high school; and three years of "young adult" senior high school.

Most important, if the mental potential and the individual behavior of each child were to be the guide to his education, he would need greater personal attention. He had to be given exactly the kind of teaching that his particular emotional, mental, and physical age called for at any one time. What was more, he had to learn by experience rather than by memorization or repetition. "Learning by doing" came to be the password. The project and the field trip were added to the more conventional learning aids—or even replaced them in the more extreme progressive schools. (Remember the similar Russian approach in the "laboratory-brigade" experiment.)

There were serious pitfalls in this new approach. Had it been applied to very small groups of children by outstanding teachers, the advantages of the new school would have been tremendous. But within the mass system, often with second-rate teachers who did not really understand the modern way, the ideal often was perverted into a fad. Instead of using projects to help the process of learning, the projects became the end of education. Understandably, parents started to worry when their youngsters knew a great deal about Indian tribes or tropical fish and little, if anything, about more important things such as arithmetic, penmanship, or English. The small groups in which children now worked together, far from assuring individual attention to each youngster, made it necessary for the teacher, whose classroom was dotted with little groups doing different things at the same time, to let the children rely on "co-operation" or group behavior. Instead of making for individual effort, this fostered conformity. In many normal youngsters it promoted good old-fashioned laziness.

At this stage, much as in the Russian school discussed in the preceding chapter, grading and competition were discouraged. Each child was to compete only with himself to the limit of his own capacity. Tests were used, not to determine achievement and effort, but to sort out children according to intelligence and potential. While the old traditional school had rigidly assumed that each child should tag along with the same fixed curriculum, the new school tended to abandon external standards.

The danger should have been obvious: the teacher presented the test score of each child as the prediction of the child's performance. While such sorting out is an enormous help in a mass-education system, it can doom the modern school to mediocrity when it is used as a crutch rather than as a guide.

This was true also of the pragmatic, or "learning by doing," technique of education. Within the framework of American society, pragmatism was inevitable. The pioneers, the railroad builders, the men who searched for the hidden treasures of gold and copper and oil were the pragmatic builders of a new society, the architects of a social philosophy that could not be proven in any way other than by action. "Does it work?" was the big question. The descendants of these philosophers of action and success created the World War II slogan: "The difficult we do at once. The impossible takes a little longer." On the education scene they had already done the impossible in record time.

But in the process of applying the "progressive" ideas to a young and still relatively unstable mass-education system, many of the most valid theories became distorted and abused.

John Dewey, probably the most misinterpreted and misquoted of all American philosophers and the convenient scapegoat for all future failures in the schools, said that education ought to be related to experience. He applied to elementary and high schools the laboratory idea of learning that had traditionally been accepted in the universities. He did not mean, despite the pronouncements of some of his more enthusiastic disciples, that experience or "doing" ought to displace all other forms of learning. He expected his students to practice teach and to work in the field. But he also lectured to them and made them study books.

When progressive educators demanded that the school educated "the whole child," they did not mean that the school ought to turn itself into a catch-all institution that would provide everything from toilet training to home economics.

They merely asked that a child's mind, his body, his environment, his hereditary advantages, and his handicaps be well considered. But too many teachers, misinterpreting the slogans, turned themselves into crank psychiatrists and into old-fashioned busybodies, ready at the drop of an undigested Freudianism to tell the parents how to run home and nursery.

"Self-expression" and "permissiveness" became the slogans of the modern school. But, here again, the difference between the original intent and the frequent perversion in practice was great. Nobody could quarrel with the doctrine that the child's expression of his own reactions is more valuable than the mere playback of memorized, undigested knowledge. But aimless expression of ignorance is probably even worse than standardized recitation: it reinforces thoughtlessness with arrogant self-reliance. There is great value in the interpretation of a child's mind and talents by means of a playful finger-painting; but it is doubtful that untutored, unguided finger painting has ever enhanced a child's artistic abilities. Place a monkey at a piano and he will probably make music. He will certainly practice self-expression. But is this education?

It is valuable, even at an early age, to give children some responsibility to govern themselves and to assume tasks that will permit them to serve society. But it is surely a perversion of the progressive idea to turn the student council into a thoughtless aping of the adult world. "Our students take their government so seriously," said the principal of a junior high school proudly. "They even buy and sell votes in their elections. They know the meaning of graft." Is such learning by doing really superior to the study of ethical concepts and of the philosophies concerning politics and human nature?

The American public became familiar with the absurdities and shook its fist at their perpetrators. More and more people laughed at the extremism as exemplified in the famous cartoon of a teacher, gagged and tied to the desk by a horde of jeering children, saying weakly: "All right, class. The lesson in self-expression is over."

Some of it was pretty silly. It offered fine material for endless debates and witty after-dinner conversation. But most of the reports themselves were exaggerated. They singled out ridiculous instances and created the impression that the entire school system of the United States had gone mad. And this is exactly the point where the Russian and the American experience must be compared. Both had adopted some of the same roads, although they were, from the outset, expected to lead to totally different goals. The American school had hoped to find a short cut to the development of the individual American within an all-inclusive mass-education system. The Soviets thought that the subordination of the school to Soviet life would lead to the creation of the new Soviet man—not an individual, exercising free and personal thought, but an efficient cog in a new social machine.

There were vast differences between the progressive Soviet school and its American counterpart. For one thing, the American educator never thought for a moment that the school should or could wither away. On the contrary, the goal was a constant strengthening and extension of the school to a point where it would affect and influence every age and every aim of the population.

Nor were the Russians' extracurricular influences, the youth brigades or the Pioneers, ever to have their counterpart in the United States. True, students were encouraged to apply their fieldwork to projects useful to the community, but there was

73

never any thought of making students an extension of the labor force. On the contrary, the American school did everything in its power to hold on to its students, with the sole purpose of furthering their education. The methods may sometimes have gone astray, but the intentions were always honorable. And it goes without saying that there was never any attempt to down-grade or degrade the teacher or use the pupils to spy on their elders.

Finally, there was this important difference: the Soviet state was able to impose the new school—the progressive experiment—totally and in complete disregard of all earlier systems and methods. It was, in Mme. Dubrovina's words, declared "correct," and overnight it became the only way, until it in turn was declared "incorrect" and replaced by a different system.

The American story was quite different. New methods were introduced experimentally and had to fight their way into the schools in competition with the traditional theories and practices of the three Rs. True, the new ideas were given powerful support by some of the strong professional organizations and by such dominating institutions as Teachers College of Columbia University. But the counterforces were always alert and ready to do battle.

For every classroom teacher who, in the overenthusiasm for an approved novelty, became uncritically progressive there was a counterweight in the good teacher in the traditional stream who, confident in her ability and knowledge, was able to distinguish between valid new discovery and dangerous quackery. For those who knew the history of education there could be little doubt about the need for more and deeper understanding of the human mind. Teachers throughout the ages had searched for it. The traditional teacher had, if he really cared about the future of his pupils, always longed for a better chance to tailor the lesson to the needs of each student. In fact, he had long envied such institutions as Oxford and Cambridge universities their "traditional" tutoring or tutorial systems. But what these teachers resisted was the misconception that children could be left to grow by themselves. They refused to believe that children could, without the benefit of wise and firm counsel, direct their own education and that the teacher should fade into the background, waiting to be asked for help.

Out of this American process of force and counterforce grew a new balance. There had been much that was sterile in the old school, often based on the lecture and memorization system of the old German classroom. The progressive "revolution" swept out the dust and the cobwebs, such as learning by rote, and forced the true values of the traditional school to defend themselves. The result is that today there are few schools in the United States that can be called all-traditional or all-progressive. The currents, after clashing head on at first, swirled around in a whirlpool of ideas, experimentation, and debate until they merged into a fusion of old and new which was different from either.

All this happened because there was not, in the United

States, any person, group, or authority that could proclaim the system "correct" or "incorrect."

The real "counterrevolution" got under way after World War II. Violent critics attacked the schools, often in search of a defenseless scapegoat for the nation's growing pains. But there were also those who, though committed heart and soul to the expansion of public education, felt that permissiveness and compromise with quality had depressed the standards of education. The forties and fifties were clearly marked by a return to a more demanding curriculum. Even before Russia's Big Red Schoolhouse burst into the headlines there were rumblings of dissatisfaction. There were demands for more and better reading, greater stress on mathematics, a return to compulsory language courses, and even some voices for the almost forgotten classics and Latin.

Purely in terms of time, the beginnings of the American and of the Russian public schools are about three quarters of a century apart. But that span of years is unimportant compared to the difference in the assignment given at first to each. The Russian schools were told to ignore all that had gone before, not only to ignore but to fight it as bourgeois and counterrevolutionary. They were ordered to create "The New Soviet Man." What that man was to be like was not to be determined by the school. His image was given *to* the school by the political masters. The purpose of the school was to find ways and means to mass-produce men in that image.

The American school, too, was to produce men who would resemble an image. The difference was that the American public schools had been given a variety of images. The workers saw the new American as a citizen in a country of truly unlimited opportunities. The school was the ladder to success. Learning would turn the entire population into a vast reservoir from which the leaders and the managers would rise. The public schools thus were expected to teach literacy in the highest sense of the word: actual literacy, of course, but only as the basis for social, political, and economic competence.

The industrialists who, during the second part of the nineteenth century, had helped to create this same public school hoped to endow it with an entirely different purpose. They wanted literacy, too; for the modern economy demanded workers of great skills. They wanted efficiency and good sense as key qualities for the labor force. But they wanted all this plus a conservative society with few, if any, changes other than efficient industrialization and merchandising.

The conflict between those two views was never completely reconciled. Even today, when taxpayers' associations fight violent battles against so-called "frills" in school expenditures, they still have in mind the limitations that would prevent the children of the "masses" from getting wrong ideas. The addition of a swimming pool to a high school may lead to the familiar campaign slogan: "Let's build schools, not country clubs." This, of course, is a way of saying that the comforts and privileges, including swimming pools, of country club life should not be made part of the school experience of too many children.

The conflict is deepened by another debate: that between the advocate of college-preparatory versus the vocational curricula. While the large cities have been able to evolve special vocational schools, specializing in the needle trades, or maritime training, or "the performing arts," the general pattern in the United States had become the "comprehensive" high school. Since these schools are held responsible for the education of all children, regardless of background or aspirations, their curriculum is easily and frequently challenged. The partisans of a "practical" education consider the academic subjects (languages, the humanities, and the social sciences) time-wasting frills likely to give youngsters "wrong ideas." On the other hand, those who believe in the civilizing values of the liberal arts, regardless of their potential for conversion into dollars, are outraged when shorthand, shop, and business English invade the curriculum. All this has often led to a compromise: the elective system, imported originally (during the first half of the century) from the German universities. Thus a great variety of courses began to be offered to the student, in addition to a certain minimum of required subjects, so that he could assemble his own program of studies. At best, with strong and compulsory guidance, this approach has worked fairly well by permitting a nonregimented type of education to be blended with the mass school. At worst, in the absence of such guidance, it has permitted youngsters to water down their education to a point of becoming a colorless, tasteless mixture devoid of intellectual vitamins.

But in spite of these conflicts, the American school grew rapidly to such strength and commanded so much popular support that, ever since the last quarter of the nineteenth century, the American high school could be certain of its goal: universality. Both elementary and high school had a sound base in the strong educational traditions, imported both from England and from the Continent, especially from Germany and France. Such nineteenth century pilot schools as Boston Latin School and Townsend Harris in New York relied on the strong classical disciplines of Latin, English, history, mathematics, and foreign languages. They started out with a fairly select group of students—not because they limited their admission but because at this stage only the abler students dared to attempt survival under the rigors of a high school education. Moreover, the domination of the European universities among the respectable professions was still so unchallenged that an American high school had to prepare an American student for later study abroad—at Berlin, Munich, Paris, or Oxford and Cambridge.

The American schools were to be given another task, unique in the history of public education: to function as the melting pot in a society that had used immigration as one of its chief sources of growth and strength. When most nations were making "likeness" a virtue and a slogan of chauvinistic pride, the United States put the very opposite—diversity—on the ideological pedestal. Out of the pogroms, famines, and persecutions of the old world came the stream of immigrants.

In retrospect, the transformation of the penniless, fear-tormented masses into the American citizenry is in itself a miracle. But the fact that within less than a generation the immigrant manpower often managed to rise above the social and economic station which its parents, grandparents, and great-grandparents had occupied in the Old Country is part of social revolution of such scope and magnitude as to be beyond comparison with any earlier upheaval in history. It could never have been achieved without the American public school. If the burden of this task, never before placed on the shoulders of any education system, slowed down the speed and quality of education and scholarship, the triumph still remains one of the baffling wonders of this age. It opened the avenues of progress in a fashion that the philosophers of democracy had dared only to dream about. The partisans of the French Revolution spilled rivers of blood in search of equality—and failed. The American public school labored, taught the untutored, pleaded with parents who failed to understand the promise of education—and succeeded.

"Where are you from," I asked a waiter, who seemed to have great difficulty with the English language.

"From Brooklyn," he said.

"Ah, yes. But before Brooklyn, where was your home?"

He said he was born in a little hamlet in Italy and had left there some twenty years ago. I asked him whether he expected, someday, to return and visit his birthplace.

"Yes," he replied. "Perhaps in two years. As soon as my

youngest boy finish college. The two younger boys—they finish already. The oldest, he will be doctor."

This is the story. Whatever may have followed, whatever may have turned out badly, the country today must not forget it. Not because it owes a debt of gratitude but because a society had set some new and lofty, yet specific, goals for the American public schools. The school made the "melting pot" an asset instead of a liability. Whether or not this achievement influenced the Russians when they demanded that their schools create the "New Soviet Man" is not certain. But there is no question that the Soviet leaders studied in close detail the American experiment in mass education. They could not have thought it a failure; for they became the second great nation (and the only other one aside from the small Scandinavian countries and, more recently, Great Britain and Israel) to imitate its universality.

Throughout the American debate and controversy, one trend remained constant: the resolute aim to make education truly universal through the high school. There may have been serious disagreement as to methods; but society by now has made up its mind that twelve years of basic schooling are the birthright of every American child. Measured in numbers only, the story is one of triumph: there are now 30,000,000 pupils in the American elementary schools and about 8,000,000 in the high schools. Every day, American school buses transport about 5,000,000 youngsters to school, which is considerably more than the entire population of Denmark.

But can numbers alone tell the story? For those who believe

it is more important to know what students learn in school than how many go to school, the following chapters will examine just what is being taught in Russia and in America and how it is being taught and what kind of citizens it creates.

Polishing Cogs
for
the Red Machine

When Mme. Dubrovina returned from her brief visit to the United States in 1956, it was her task, as Deputy Minister of Education, to direct the rewriting of the Soviet textbooks. De-Stalinization was at its height. The "cult of personality" was being attacked from all directions, and although university students in Tiflis were rumored to have been rioting in defense of Stalin, the new direction seemed to be generally accepted and greeted as a possible step toward the relaxing of the controls of the police state.

But if the textbooks were being purged, there was no indication that the goal which Stalin had set for the schools in the late twenties was undergoing any change. That goal was clearly and directly to turn the Soviet Union into a great industrial power. Stalin had proclaimed his target long before Russia became a victim of German aggression. When he later instructed his Foreign Secretary Molotov to sign a treaty of co-operation with Nazi Germany, it must have occured to him that a combination of the industrial might of Germany, Russia, and Imperial Japan would eventually forge a block of such incomparable economic strength that it would be difficult to challenge its political and military power.

The dream was temporarily shattered by the German attack. But postwar history, with its spectacular progress of Soviet industrial power, has undoubtedly revived it, with the addition of the manpower and resources of the East European satellites and with the growing potential of Red China. Though the figures are not completely reliable, the 1958 steel production of the Soviet-Chinese block may have equaled the production of the United States. Russia's new Prime Minister and Communist Party head Nikita Khruschev bluntly told the Western nations: "We will bury you," adding that he expected to accomplish this victory through industrial and economic competition. Soviet rocketry, the successful launching of the earth satellites, and the demonstration of Soviet passenger jet planes all have emphasized to the world that the threat and the achievements are not bluff or empty boast. They are real.

Equally real was the shock in the United States.

The schools of the Soviet Union had long been ridiculed. It was silently agreed that the United States held the patent to mass education. No dictatorship could even vaguely compete in the battle of education with the power of the free mind, schooled in institutions that were protected by the guarantees of academic freedom.

The industrial product of the Soviet Union, too, had been laughed at. The Russian luxury car, the American press liked to point out, was nothing but a carbon copy of an outdated model of the Packard. American industry, and presumably the government officials who gave their blessing to the stunt, were so sure of United States superiority that a "secret shipment" containing the 1957 Ford was dispatched to Moscow before its American unveiling to startle the Russian masses.

When the Soviet air force flew a formation of long-range jet bombers—rumored to be superior to the American counterpart—across Red Square, in ostentatiously full view of Western diplomats, a United States expert shrugged them off as mere propaganda prototypes which could not be mass-produced for a long time, if ever, in backward Russian factories.

Even when Sputnik was put in orbit, the habit of complacency seemed so ingrained that a high-ranking American official referred to it as a bauble. President Eisenhower said initially that the achievement did not alter his thoughts about United States technological superority by "one iota."

But the public no longer listened to the soothing voices of the official spokesmen. The public was shocked. Comfortable theories seemed badly out of focus. The earlier Russian claims that practically all the instruments of modern technology—from the telephone to the plane—had really been invented by Russians no longer seemed so hilarious.

Understandably the shock led public opinion to the other extreme. Complacency gave way to panic. The search was on for the source of the Russian success, and since the American public has been taught to believe in the supreme power of education, it was concluded that the Soviet school must now be superior to the American school. If not superior, it must, at least, have been training a generation of men and women to be reckoned with.

What is this new Soviet school, which Stalin ordered to produce the human material for an industrialized Russia, really like? What does it demand of its students? What does it teach them?

The basic Russian school—the equivalent of the twelve years of public schooling that is the normal education offered to American students—is the ten-year school. It is still in the process of being made universal, with the target date on which it should be available to all children set for 1960. (Even this statement must be modified: not all Soviet children are given the opportunity to advance through all stages of public school, and most recent developments may lead to a cutback to only seven years of universal schooling.)

The total course is subdivided into three phases, not too different from the organization of the American elementary, junior high, and high school. Grades one to four roughly resemble the grade school; grades five through seven (incomplete secondary school) introduce some of the more difficult elements of learning; grades eight through ten (complete secondary school) were originally thought to be college preparatory and led to a maturity or school-leaving examination which could be roughly compared to the high school diploma. Actually it is a cross between the latter and the European examination, which qualifies the student for university admission.

When the Russian seven-year old begins school in the first grade, his opening weeks are not too different from the same stretch in the life of his slightly younger (about six years old) American counterpart. Like the American youngster, he may or may not have gone to kindergarten—in fact the likelihood that he has not attended kindergarten is slightly greater. There is a considerable shortage of kindergartens in Russia and attendance is not free.

Outwardly there is a big difference: wherever textile production has caught up with the demand, Soviet pupils—both boys and girls in the now predominately co-educational schools—wear uniforms. The little girls' attire is a slightly more drab version, if this is possible, than the uniforms of the old British private schools. The boys sport a visored cap and a vaguely military outfit with knee pants.

The first few weeks might be summed up with the American catchall phrase of "orientation." The teacher tells the youngsters about the school, about the things they should and should not do, about the proper way of asking questions. Almost at once, the teaching of the alphabet begins. In contrast with the new American method, which tries to get youngsters ready for reading and writing and which works "backwards," beginning with pictures and entire words, Russia has stuck to the traditional way. Individual letters are "learned" and practiced; words are formed, containing the familiar letters; "new" words are broken down through recognition of the familiar letters, and the sounds of the letters lead to the discovery of new words.

At the end of first grade the Russian pupil is expected to be able to read and write simple texts and to be ready to move on, in grade two, to extensive spelling practice and to the basic knowledge of the rules of grammar.

The Soviet pupils who finish elementary school, through grade four, are expected to read easy texts, many of them with a strongly scientific slant, written especially for this age group. They are given simple compositions and letters to write and they are frequently tested on the clarity of their speech and expression.

American children in those early grades are generally offered reading matter especially prepared for them, ranging from Mother Goose and childish adventure to a certain new type of meaningless double talk "scientifically" designed by education specialists ("Mary sees John. John sees Mary. Where is John? He is here."). Russian youngsters in the early grades get acquainted with Russian folk stories as well as with such authors as Pushkin, Tolstoi, Gorki, and Fadeev. How much of this reading they actually understand is debatable and depends on the skill of the teacher. At any rate, even these little pupils are required to memorize long passages of Soviet and Russian literature, fables, and folklore. The first reaction is to blame this on the foibles and weaknesses of autocratic Soviet education. But this is not strictly so. It is rather in the European tradition, which always prided itself in making children "perform" and which has long subscribed to the theory that the human mind can be trained early by memorization, even if the capacity to understand still lags far behind.

American educators, ironically, consider this view ultra-reactionary, and so did the early Soviet school after the Revolution. In fact, such current methods would not have displeased the Czarist Ministers of Education. This, in turn, does not mean that it is all wrong or that the American disdain for memory work in grade school is the ultimate achievement of modern progress. Anyone who has watched children, even below school age, enjoy the fun of mimicry and their facility for imitation knows that this is an ability that ought to be exploited. The question is the extent to which the child's mind is able to follow the thoughts and meaning of the memorized passages. If memorization is purely mechanical, it not only is useless but can become harmful. The child in the traditional American school who sings day after day "My country is a tree" is worse off than the child who has never memorized the song.

The point is that understanding and memorization need not be mutually exclusive. If the two can be combined, the result is good. Children recite nursery rhymes long before they know how to read. There is no reason why this aspect of the brain's work should suddenly be stopped, only to be started again later, say in school dramatics, when memorizing becomes absolutely necessary.

In its renewed stress on "memory work" the Russian school is not opening up new territory. On the contrary, it merely returned to the European pattern of education. Every French and German elementary school pupil proudly recites the required number of poems and frequently is expected to commit even outstanding prose passages to memory.

Nor are the beginnings of the Russian child's mathematical learning peculiarly Russian. In the first four grades the Russian child is required to learn addition, subtraction, multiplication, and division of whole numbers, addition and subtraction of fractions, concepts of time, and the metric system. In the latter, incidentally, the Russian child has the easier course open to all children, except those in Britain and the United States, where custom, tradition, and a certain amount of cultural pigheadedness have preserved a totally impractical and unwieldly system of yards, feet, inches, and irregular pounds.

Undoubtedly there are some American schools that accomplish a rigorous mission similar to the one set for teachers by the Russian elementary school. But by and large the initial Russian learning requirements are stiffer, and they are more uniform than they are in the United States. Whether this is an advantage or a handicap will be examined later.

The beginnings of science teaching in the Russian elementary school are not very different from those of the American counterpart. The original purpose is to awaken children's interest in nature and give them some inkling of the ways in which nature works: how one season follows the other; what the sun and water and fire do for the world and its people; what the process of eating and the growing of food mean to the life of animals and human beings. Not unlike the American grade school, the Russian classroom may have its pet goldfish and turtles. A not uncommon adjunct to classroom learning is the garden plot, or at least a few window boxes for the less fortunate city children.

Russian children do, however, enter into a far more systematic study of natural science considerably earlier than do most American youngsters. In fourth grade they are introduced to the basic study of water, air, soil, minerals, and the scientific problems of change. Here again it is difficult to make any exact comparison with the American school—so much depends on the individual teacher and on the school system—but it is safe to say that few American children reach this level of learning and instruction before the beginning of junior high school, or the seventh grade.

Even taking into consideration that the American first grader starts school at about one year younger, the Russian child begins basic instruction in natural science two years earlier than his American counterpart. What is more significant, the natural science course in fourth grade is merely the prelude to an organized three-year elementary science curriculum that starts in fifth grade. It includes laboratory work, practical, semi-scientific gardening, and meaningful observation through a microscope.

More telling than the specific content of the first few years of teaching in the Soviet school is the oragnization of that system. The European tradition generally has followed a division of four years of elementary school and anywhere from six to nine years of secondary school. In the German

93

system, which has probably been the most important influence on the Russian school, four years of elementary school were followed either by another four years or compulsory non-academic *Volkschule* or "people's school," or by various types of selective secondary schooling, most of it college preparatory, at least in theory. After a fairly stiff achievement test, the academic student went on to another six years of high school work oriented in three different directions in three different types of school:

1. The Humanist Gymnasium, in the classical or humanistic tradition, with great stress on Latin (eight years), Greek (three to four years), and the sweep of history from ancient Greece to modern Europe, but with relatively little emphasis on the sciences, except in a theoretical, historical sense.

2. The Real Gymnasium, representing a fusion of the classical and the modern curriculum which eliminated Greek and reduced the Latin requirements (to about three to four years) in favor of a good deal of modern language study, a heavy load of mathematics and science.

3. The Reform Gymnasium, which took the completely "Modernized" road that combined modern language, modern social studies, and mathematics with a good deal of practical prevocational and business studies.

While all three streams could lead into the universities, the first usually aimed at the more purely academic careers, the second prepared mainly for scientific and engineering study, and the third most frequently led into the higher business careers, often preceded by university work in business administration, statistics, or management.

In either of the three streams, the six years after elementary school were considered an educational entity, and the student was able to drop out at the end of the sixth year with the semblance of a completed high school education. Only those who definitely aimed at higher education remained after the sixth year. Under the old plan, there followed three more college preparatory years, with academic work resembling that of the first two years of an American college. During the Hitler regime, a so-called "school reform" reduced those final years to two, largely because of the rapidly growing demands of the armed forces, both for plain manpower and for officer material. The final year of secondary school (which at this point resembles the level of secondary school in most European countries, including France, Belgium, Holland, and Scandinavia) is concluded with an extremely thorough series of written and oral achievement examinations or maturity test—the *Abitur* in Germany or the *baccalauréat* in France —which is also the university admission test.

The American school has abandoned this type of organization almost completely. Originally it extended the period of elementary school from the European four-year stretch to eight years; followed by four years of high school. Why? There were a number of reasons, none of them specifically stated. The basic reason, probably, was that, in the revolutionary attempt to make education compulsory and universal, it was easier to start with a vast extension of elementary school. It was easier, first of all, to work out a curriculum for this great mass of children; but it was probably even more important to devise a system for which teachers could be found. The more or less hastily established two-year normal schools, which often turned out teachers who were not very far above the level of knowledge of the ordinary high school graduate, were at least capable of providing elementary schools with teachers. Where should the country have found the teachers for an eight- or nine-year high school?

But there was probably another important factor in the American extension of the elementary school period. American educators and parents embraced the relatively new theory that children should not be pushed too hard, that the education of the human body and mind should closely parallel their natural development. Anyone who has attended a European high school—and remember that the child entered secondary education roughly at age ten or eleven—knows that neither its curriculum nor its teachers were willing to make many concessions to the immaturity of the adolescent, much less the childish mind. The average university-educated European high school "professor" tends to look on his class as on a privileged group of youngsters permitted to benefit from his wisdom. He is the scholar. They are the uneducated, and they are to be divided into the group of the smart and willing on the one side and the dumb or unwilling on the other.

An illustration, though perhaps an exaggerated one, was the gymnasium classroom in a German city shortly after World War II. The teacher was going through the morning's lesson in German literature. He was "dissecting" poetry and questioning the class on both content and style. After the bell rang, the teacher turned apologetically to the foreign visitor. "You must not consider this class typical," he said. "Many of them are stupid and should not be here. But some of them are veterans, soldiers who were in the war, and we must now offer them a high school education. But they do not really belong here because they are stupid."

The United States, in establishing eight years of elementary school, sharply broke with the tradition of the unbending scholar-teacher, who set up standards to suit himself and the system—and the "stupid" student be damned. American educators and parents were convinced that it was wrong to treat ten-year-olds as though they were miniature adults. They not only looked like children, they were children, and the school would have to take this truth into consideration.

Guided by this new philosophy, American schools rushed all the way to the opposite extreme. In fact, the great majority of educators soon began to suspect this themselves, and in the rethinking of the ideal school pattern they generally abandoned the eight-year elementary school. The key to this rethinking was the new knowledge gleaned from the new science of child psychology and from the study of the stages of development of the human mind and body. The problem was how to separate not only children from "young students" but to make the additional break between boys and girls on the one hand and adolescents on the other.

Thus the junior high school was born. Two years were

chopped off the elementary school and one year off the high school, and there was interposed between six years of grade school and three years of high school that three-year stretch comprising a totally new educational animal: the junior high school. Its purpose was to find a place—safe and pro-tected—for the group of youngsters who were no longer children and not yet adolescents. The aim was to cushion the transition and absorb the shock that comes with the inevitable move from childish play-learning to real study. Whether or not this experiment has turned out to be a success, it was unique.

Or was it? The generally unrecognized fact is that the Russian system, which in so many ways follows the lines of traditional European education, here veered away from Germany and France—and accepted a good deal of the American example. The division of the school into six years of elementary, three years of junior high, and three years of high school emerged in the Russian adaptation as four years of elementary school, three years of the equivalent of junior high school and three years of college-preparatory senior high school. None of these terms is usually used in Western descriptions of the Russian ten-year school, but the resemblance is unmistakable.

So much for the resemblance. What about the differences? The obvious one is that of the two "missing" years in the Soviet elementary school. Is this a weakness? Is it only a temporary expedient? (Don't forget that the Soviet ten-year school is still a goal rather than an accomplished fact—

with the target year of its completion set for 1960 and the actual achievement likely to be cancelled by Khrushchev's "School reform.") The answer is "no." The four-year elementary school is neither weakness nor expedient. Based on observation in Europe, the Russians have good reason to be convinced that four years of grade school is sufficient. They probably feel that an extension of elementary education beyond those four years would be a waste of time, a watering-down. Proof for this theory is the fact that the Russians have begun to talk about the expansion of the ten-year school into an eleven- or even twelve-year system; but in planning the extra years, they inevitably say that the additions will be made to the high school end of the education scheme.

Here the Russian view coincides with the opinion of many critics of the current American system. There is a growing feeling, even among more conventional American educators, that the American school has permitted elementary school to be strung out too long and to spread itself too thin. Since much—if not most—of the grade school program is devoted to the teaching of the basic skills, the question is whether a shortening of the stretch would not improve rather than weaken the over-all fabric of education. The defenders of the "slow-growth" concept reply that there are many intangibles that the American elementary school must teach—getting along with groups, understanding other children, developing new tastes and a curiosity for further exploration and learning. But do these intangibles need to be tied to a six-year elementary school? May not the lack of intellectual stimulus dull a child's natural hunger to learn?

There is, however, another important difference—in addition to mere timing. More and more teachers and parents in America complain that the junior high school fails to set clearly defined goals for itself. Originally meant to be a transition from playing to serious study, from the learning of basic skills to the understanding of more specialized knowledge, the junior high school is frequently accused of being no more than a beefed-up continuation of grade school. In plain terms, it often is neither fish nor fowl. Instead of absorbing the shock of transition, it may blot out the excitement and the mystery of moving from one stage of learning to another.

The Russian fifth grade, if it is to be looked at as the beginning of junior high school, opens to the pupil (who is about eleven years old, compared with the thirteen-year-old American seventh grader) a truly new world of learning. He has been given a slight taste of what was to come when in the last year of elementary school (fourth grade). This consists of two hours each of history, geography, and biology added to the regular grade school fare of Russian, arithmetic, art, singing, and physical education. Whereas in the earlier grades, history and geography have been part of the general reading and writing curriculum, just as they are in any good elementary school in the United States, in Russian fourth grade they assume the status of a subject. It goes without saying that such instruction follows the ideological line of the

Communist state. History, from the outset, is taught, not as the chronicle of relations between men, people, and nations, but as the battleground of classes and the evolution of a social structure. To the planner of the New Soviet Man the question is not whether the fourth-grade child is too young to be indoctrinated. The question is rather whether he is young enough. The interpretation of Soviet society must be laid *before* the teaching of anything else can seriously begin. It is the cornerstone. It is true that this ideological teaching indoctrination will continue throughout the various levels of schooling, but the important point, often overlooked by American observers, is that the early and basic teaching of this biased view of the world permits a great deal of *real*, effective, and intellectually tough teaching from then on. Too many Western theorists have deluded themselves into thinking that the Soviet system devotes so much time to pure indoctrination as to be educationally self-defeating. This is not so. True, the indoctrination and the bias are never permitted to be relaxed, but it is equally true that they are not permitted to interfere with the process of a rigorous, demanding education.

At any rate, when the Russian youngster enters fifth grade —call it junior high school—he is ready for a curriculum of study which includes (weekly) nine hours of Russian language and literature; six hours of mathematics; two hours of history; three hours of geography; two hours of biology; two hours of physical education; two hours of some form of practical work, either on the farm or in a workshop; and one hour each of art and music. But—and this may be among the most important hints to the substance and promise of the Russian junior high school—he is also introduced to a foreign language and devotes four hours a week to its study.

This is a crucial point of difference and comparison. In all the other areas the prejudiced defender of the American system can successfully argue that the truly good and successful American elementrary school, given good teachers, does cover much of the specific subject matter of these various disciplines, without calling them by their technical and scholarly name. But the introduction of a foreign language at an age level which, in the American school, would very definitely be part of the elementary grades shows that the Russian school—intellectually speaking—means business. Nor can this be shrugged off with the reply that teaching certain things at too early an age can be harmful. In fact the best among the American schools are now trying to revise their curriculum to include foreign language instruction on the elementary level, and those few that have tried this have reported it to be highly successful.

The teaching of a foreign language at this early stage, to be carried through the entire ten-year school curriculum, shows that the Russian school has made great progress in the use of long-range and continuing study of a subject. In contrast to the American student, who often selects one language (usually not before seventh or eighth grade) and, for various reasons, may switch to another language two years later without continuing the study of the first one, the average Russian student is likely to end up with a good working knowledge of either French, German, English or Spanish. If he is bright, he will have real fluency.

The "continuing" approach again is not a Russian invention. It is based on the traditional experience of the European school. The Russian school has added to it the early start, which, especially in the study of a language, exploits the young child's superior power of mimicry and his lack of adolescent inhibitons. The result is that some 40 per cent of Russia's high school graduates finish with a pretty thorough knowledge of English, 40 per cent know German, and the remainder have studied either French, Spanish, or, in a few instances, Latin.

This is a long way from the typical American story, told by the late columnist Heywood Broun, who said that he had taken beginner's French in school but found out, when he first got to Paris, that nobody in France speaks beginner's French.

The point is that, with the beginning of fifth grade (the junior high school equivalent), the Russian school veers sharply away from elementary school practice and content while the American school, even in the seventh grade (its beginning of junior high school), still hesitates to make the break with childhood and to move into the early stages of "studentship."

In sixth grade, the Russian school adds to its biology teaching two hours per week of a second science—physics—while reducing only the Russian language and literature instruction by one hour, from nine to eight hours a week.

In seventh grade all the earlier subjects continue on the study plan, but with another reduction of Russian by two hours. On the other hand, biology and physics are both increased from two hours to three, with the addition of two hours of chemistry and one hour of technical drawing. Foreign language instruction is reduced from four to three hours and both art and singing are dropped from the curriculum altogether, apparently as the last holdover from the elementary school curriculum. By this time the Russian student is deep in the study of algebra and geometry, but he has also by the end of the seventh grade covered the history of mankind from the prehistoric period and the ancient Orient through Greece, Rome, the Middle Ages, and up to "The English Bourgeois Revolution of 1648."

That this is not history of the kind that would be taught in an American school (if it were taught there at all) goes without saying. In fact, the basis for the "correct" interpretation of history is firmly implanted in the Soviet child's mind *before* that mind can possibly formulate any independent judgment. In fourth grade, after a brief summary of Russian history, children are told how the Communist party led the workers to their liberation and how Lenin brought about the Bolshevik Revolution. This is the framework. The early indoctrination acts as a focus for every aspect of personal interpretation and thought that is bound to follow as the child grows into the stages of advancing maturity and independent thinking. But the fact to keep in mind, too, is that once the framework has been built, the Russian school moves on in a very businesslike manner. It never seems to forget the demand made by Stalin in 1928: the goal is an accumulation of knowledge.

Continuing the progress up the Russian ladder of learning (and using American terminology for purposes of easy comparison only), the Russian student enters senior high school in his eighth grade. He is now about fourteen years old as compared with the American fifteen-year-old who begins senior high school in tenth grade if his community subscribes to the modern plan of six years of elementary, three years of junior high, and three years of high school. If he is part of an old-fashioned eight-four school district, he would enter high school at about the age of fourteen at the ninth grade level. But his previous education would have been entirely in the elementary school, which means that few, if any, of his teachers were highly trained specialists in their subject matter.

The Russian high school student switches from Russian Language entirely to literature, an indication that, at least in theory, he is expected to have mastered the technique of grammar by that time. If this is true in practice, it is a notable advance over the achievement of the American high school. In fact, even the routine freshman English course in the best of the American colleges still devotes a major part of its first term to grammar and writing practice. Because of neglect in the high schools, a majority of America's colleges and universities are forced to offer special courses in remedial English in order to bring their students up to acceptable standards in the use of their native language. Recently the dean of the Columbia University Law School complained that even law students were still deficient in the use of simple English. There is no question whatsoever that the Soviet student, on entering higher education, is completely familiar with the details of the elaborate grammar and vocabulary of his mother tongue.

In his eighth grade the Russian student continues to devote about six hours a week to mathematics, a pace he will maintain through ninth and tenth grades. In addition he studies history for four hours, which he will do for the remainder of high school, geography for about two to three hours during eighth and ninth grades, and his foreign language for three weekly lessons each school year.

His science requirements permit biology to taper off to two hours in eighth grade and one hour in ninth; physics, on the other hand, builds up from three hours in eighth grade to four hours in ninth and better than five hours a week in the "senior year." He keeps up his weekly hour of technical drawing and two hours of physical education and adds, in his final year, one hour each in astronomy, psychology and—by way of a last-minute reminder of the power and requirements of the State—the Constitution of the Soviet Union. Even in his practical work, stepped up to two hours a week during the entire three-year period, he has now advanced to such intricate areas as machine construction and electro-technology, at least if he is a city boy.

Much the same curriculum applies, if the student happens to be a city girl. There is probably less sex classification of occupations and careers, and therefore of subject matter, in Russia than in any other country, an important consideration in any calculation of the total reservoir of skills in the Soviet manpower pool.

We have now followed the "typical" Soviet youngster through the ten-year school. We have an idea—if only a very sketchy one—as to the total curriculum offered to him and the type of knowledge expected of him. We know that all his learning is shaped and fashioned by the first and foremost demand of the State: to create the new Soviet man. We know that in the humanities there is no chance for the pupil to try to arrive at a philosophy of life or at an independent interpretation of history. The philosophy of life is simply that of serving the Soviet State and its aims, and to adjust to its changing short-range targets; the interpretation of history is that handed down by Marx and Lenin and amended, at irregular intervals, by the Supreme Soviet and by the masters of the State. But we also know that in the sciences there are no dictates other than those to produce: to produce knowledge and thus be able to further the economic and military strength of the Soviet State.

These are not acceptable aims of education in the American or Western democratic meaning of the word; but the fact to remember is that they are aims which education can be made to serve effectively and efficiently. They must, therefore, be taken seriously. In the remaining chapters these aims will be treated as an inescapable fact, not (as has been our custom in the past) as an inevitable handicap or (as we now so frequently assume) as a natural advantage.

A crucial question, so far unanswered, is to what extent, and how effectively, this program of education is applied to the Russian child. How many Russian children are actually reached by it?

5

Honors and Flunking—
East and West

A recent issue of *Life* magazine featured on its cover the pictures of two teen-agers. One was a high school student in Moscow; the other a high school teen-ager in the United States. The description of the two boys' studies and interests made it obvious that the Soviet student would eventually excel as a brilliant, highly skilled, thoroughly educated citizen, probably a scientist. The American emerged as a likable, reasonably literate, though by no means outstanding, person to whom, at best, the description "well-rounded" might be attached.

An American educator, himself a leader in the drive to improve the standards of American schools, dismissed the comparison by suggesting that the feature story compared an average American student with the Russian equivalent of an American Phi Beta Kappa honor student.

We will never be able to determine completely whether the alarming magazine comparison or the educator's reservations are closer to the mark. But, on the basis of some fairly conclusive evidence, we should be able to make a reliable estimate.

The basic difficulty is that, first, Soviet statistics are both incomplete and highly "colored." They suffer not only from a very constant attempt to turn every fact and figure into an instrument of propaganda, but they are distorted by administrative inefficiencies that are not surprising in such a vast and recently centralized country. It is hard to tell whether the frantic and sometimes truly comic attempts to cover up inadequacies is a Soviet innovation or whether it is borrowed from the tradition of the East-European bureaucracies. After all, the false façades of the Potemkin village made worldwide history long before there was a Ministry of Information. In the course of a state visit to Belgrade by Ethiopian Emperor Haile Selassie only a few years ago, each peasant along the route from the airport to the city was given just enough orange paint to spruce up the front of his farmhouse. And so it is not really surprising (but worthy of a constant mental exclamation point) that almost every educational reference by American visitors to the Soviet Union concerns Moscow's ten-year school No. 201. It is, by American standards, an adequate school, with good, though by no means elaborate, equipment. We can safely assume that it represents one of the best of the Russian schools, at least in terms of appearance and equipment. We can only guess how much worse other Russian schools might be. But for a realistic estimate of some of the weaknesses and strong points of Soviet education, there are a number of strong hints and vital observations for which no secret intelligence is needed.

Whenever I entered a New York public school classroom together with Mme. Dubrovina, the Deputy Minister of Education for the Federated Soviet Socialist Republic, among her first questions was invariably: "How many of this class are expected to fail?" Even in first or second grade she expected that only a certain percentage would make the grade.

In this question is an important clue to a vital aspect of the Soviet school system. It takes a completely different slant on the idea of universal mass education than does the American school. Instead of being all-inclusive, ready to graduate every student who is willing to "sit it out," it is highly selective. The question is: how selective and what are the criteria of selection?

Here Mme. Dubrovina offered another hint. She was fascinated by even the most fundamental intelligence and aptitude tests. After some preliminary discussion of different types of tests, she admitted that the Soviet schools had stopped using any such tests when they "reformed" their system in 1928—or, more accurately, when they returned to traditional methods. So thorough was the return to the past that even the progress made in modern testing and in the new-found means of measuring students' potential talents was discarded.

The only tests used henceforth in the Soviet Union were "achievement tests," which examined the student on the basis of what he had already learned and graded him accordingly. And as such marks and tests were reintroduced, they were let loose on the Soviet student with a vengeance. In the course of the ten-year school, a student had to pass about forty-four "final" or major examinations—each of them important in determining whether or not the student would go on to the next higher step on the education ladder. It was only in 1954, and apparently after the beginnings of serious complaints by teachers, parents, and even medical authorities, that the heavy load was slightly reduced to an average of twenty-six "finals" in a Soviet student's career.

The examination became a dread instrument that verged on persecution, not only for the student, but for the teacher as well. Teachers were judged in accordance with their students' ability to pass examinations, and the inevitable happened. Teachers "cheated" in grading students' papers. One refugee who had been a high school teacher in Soviet Russia before World War II reported that most teachers passed at least 90 per cent of their class, while, if graded "properly," almost 50 per cent might have flunked. The situation became so ludicrous that, after several years of unsuccessful threats, attempts at supervision, and spot checks, the authorities admitted defeat and ceased to judge teachers by the "success" of their students in examinations.

In recent years the Soviets have not published detailed percentage figures of success and failure, but the continued severity of the tests and the exclusive reliance on "achievement" tests make it clear that the essential story is still the same as indicated by the prewar tabulations. These figures give the lie to any claim of truly universal mass education.

By the end of fourth grade—which means at the conclusion of grade school—slightly more than half of the students who had entered the public schools at the age of seven had already dropped out. Translated into American terms, fewer than half of the children were given the opportunity of ever entering junior high school.

From here on, the dropout rate mounted even more rapidly. At the next important "break," the end of seventh grade, only slightly more than 15 per cent of the entire group of children were left. Or, to use the familiar term again, at roughly the equivalent of the beginning of senior high school, 85 per cent of the particular age group of Soviet children had already forfeited their chance. When final graduation rolled around, only 4.5 per cent were left to claim their diplomas.

These are key figures to any attempt to understand the Soviet school and, especially, to any valid comparison with the American system. In the United States, at the conclusion of twelve years of public school, about 55 per cent of the entire age group are graduated—compared with 4.5 per cent in Russia. And even this tells only part of the story; for while only half of all Soviet children go beyond the four years of grade school, almost 100 per cent of all American children finish at least the six years of elementary school. Against roughly 15 per cent of Russian adolescents who enter senior high school, furthermore, must be charged the approximately 85 per cent of American youngsters who take part, at least, in the beginnings of high school.

These figures, admittedly, are based on prewar Soviet statistics. There have been changes, but these were not in effect before 1954. Since then, largely because of a relaxation of the examination requirements and a slight watering down of the curriculum, especially in mathematics and science, the total percentage of high school graduates is reported to have risen to about 12 or 15 per cent of the entire age group of young boys and girls, compared to the prewar 4.5 per cent.

What does this mean? It means in very plain and simple terms that the Soviet Union does not have a mass-education system as we understand it. The Russian school, in fact, comes much closer to being a modified version of the traditional European school, modified largely by the American concept of school structure. In the light of the facts and figures, the Soviet claim of having built a universal mass-education system is false. What the Soviets have established—and in terms of their historic background and limitations this is a remarkable achievement—is a system of public education which permits every child to enter elementary school and which virtually guarantees every child's right to basic literacy as well as to *competition* for the right to secondary education.

This is a great deal, and it has given the Soviet Union a literacy rate approximately equal to that of the United States. But beyond this point, the Soviet school is about as selective as the German or the French school—and not nearly so demanding in terms of quality. Germany and France, before World War II, graduated approximately 7 to 8 per cent of its youth from its 8- or 9-year secondary schools. The percentage today is approximately 12 to 15 per cent. It would therefore be more realistic to compare the Russian and the European school systems rather than the Soviet and the American achievement.

What the Russians are trying to do, largely for reasons of ideology and propaganda, is to pretend that they have beaten the United States at its own game. What is more, the Russians, for obvious and, from their own point of view, sound reasons did not play the same game. For better or for worse, the American school has assumed that the entire youth of the nation can be made to fit into the over-all framework of a total mass-education system. The American school planned, experimented, and struggled to prove this revolutionary theory feasible. Whether the revolution and the experiment have been a failure or a success is not at issue at this point of the discussion. The fact is that the Russian school, despite its claim of equal opportunity and its surface guise of American-style mass education, has done no more and no less than to serve the aims and purposes of its own philosophy: to provide the required number of educated men and women to carry out the plans and functions determined by the State. One of the urgent demands made by the State was the creation of a manpower reservoir of high efficiency and technical excellence. The school's major function was the education of that group. To those who failed to make the grade the State and the school felt no direct educational obligation.

What happens to those who fail—this large number of

Russian boys and girls whom, if they had been born Americans, the American school would feel obliged to pull along and to push forward to higher achievement, greater competency, and a better share of personal security and happiness?

The Soviets had to ask themselves that question as their public schools expanded. By 1940 they had reached the point where the alternatives were to follow the American course of trying to fit the entire vast population into the expanding system of elementary and high schools or to throw democratic ideals to the wind and take the easy road of being selective and exclusive. It was an easy decision for a political system which, except for propaganda purposes, has little regard for the individual human being. And so, by a decree of October 2, 1940, the government authorized an annual "draft" of between 800,000 to 1,000,000 "males fourteen to seventeen years of age" for a period of training that varied from six months to two years, depending on the skills required, and was to be followed by four years of compulsory work duty. Shortly thereafter the draft was extended to include girls between the ages of sixteen and eighteen. In 1947 the "draft age" for girls was lowered to fifteen. Between the years 1940 to 1956, according to a report in *Pravda* of August 20, 1956, more than 8,000,000 youths had been trained in the Labor Reserve Schools. The target for the 1955 to 1960 period for these institutions is "3,500,000 more such workers for industry, transportation, construction, and agriculture."

The Labor Reserve School, which siphons off great numbers of preadolescents roughly at the junior high school level, provides training on a level incomparably lower than the American vocational school. It is essentially an instrument to feed semiskilled labor into industry and to transfer great numbers of surplus farm children into the industrial urban centers. Soviet semantics, by glorifying the achievement of these involuntary workers, pretends that the Labor Reserve Schools are a legitimate part of the public education system. On February 15, 1947, for instance, *Pravda* boasted that "pupils in labor schools produced 2,000,000 tons of coal and 270,000 tons of ore, overhauled and repaired 2000 locomotives and 17,000 freight cars, built 2000 metalworking machines, and made 60,000,000 rubles' worth of spare parts for agricultural machinery." In two years alone—1947 and 1948—these schools sent about 690,000 young boys into the coal mines.

These youngsters are taken out of the stream of real education at a very early age—roughly at about thirteen or fourteen years—and on the basis only of achievement tests. This means that the large group of intelligent boys and girls, who mature more slowly and who, in the United States, have often been shown to overtake the "early bloomers," are never given a chance. They are switched on a dead-end siding, without any opportunity to rise either in education or in status. Their sole purpose from here on is to serve as useful, productive manpower.

A slightly higher standard of training applies to the new technical trades schools, established in 1954, which provide the Soviet economy with machine operators, mechanics, plumbers, draftsmen, and other skilled personnel and even junior supervisors in some 100 occupational categories. At the latest count in 1956, there were 439 technical trades schools, with a total enrollment of just below 120,000.

Finally, there is a limited number of schools which prepare engineering technicians, the technikums. Some students may enter these schools at the end of their seven-year school, thus completing their high school education in institutions that are a mixture of vocational high school and subengineering education. These schools offer from two to four years of instruction and may lead to a type of two-year technical institute of higher education that would be comparable to the American junior college.

It is never easy to compare the educational institutions of one country with those of another. Under the immediate shock of recognition that the Soviet Union had come of age as an industrial power, it was natural that headlines, magazine articles, and political speeches would try to simplify the competitive aspects of the Soviet and the American education systems in such easily understood statistics as the number of students enrolled in Soviet engineering institutions and the American equivalents.

The trouble is that the figures given for the Russian technikums are misleading. At present, enrollment in these institutions is stabilized somewhere near one million students. Some of the technikums, including the one at Kiev to which United States visitors are invariably taken, undoubtedly come close to the quality of instruction offered at some American engineering colleges. But these are the exception rather than the rule.

The most descriptive summary of the difference is given by Nicholas DeWitt, of the Russian Research Center at Harvard University in his book, *Soviet Professional Manpower*:

"An American machine-shop foreman may be a person who has acquired his skill through experience, while the same occupation in the Soviet Union may be filled by a person who was graduated from an industrial technikum and who specialized, let us say, in the design, maintenance, and operation of machine tools. Our electronics technician may be a graduate of a trade school or he may have taken some apprentice courses conducted by a large manufacturer. An electronics technician in the Soviet Union is likely to be a graduate of an electrical engineering technikum. Our nurses receive a certificate from an accredited hospital or possibly a college degree, while the Soviet nurse is a secondary medical school graduate. Our veterinarian is often an agricultural college major, while in the Soviet Union he is likely to be a veterinarian technikum graduate. Soviet dentists are primarily graduates of secondary specialized schools of dental medicine. Our railroad traffic dispatchers probably receive on-the-job training, while in the Soviet Union they are transportation technikum graduates. Our primary school teacher is probably a teachers college graduate, while the Soviet elementary school teacher is likely to be a pedagogical school graduate. Our technical draftsman is probably an industrial high school graduate. In the Soviet Union the same skill is acquired in an engineering technikum."

The question then remains whether the Soviet idea of specialization and specialized training through the schools is a temporary expedient, dictated by the economic facts of the present stage of Russian development, or an ideological preference. Is it, in other words, an extension of the early Marxist forecast that the school would become a mere preparation for the factory? Or is it the result of the limitations of a very newly industrialized society? It may well be true that the American way of relying on the skilled foreman for specialized teaching would be impossible to pursue in a country that is still desperately short of highly skilled foremen. The Russian program of industrialization, with its high-pressure goals set by Stalin and probably intensified by the post-Stalin regimes, frankly and unhesitatingly uses the school, especially the technikum, as a "crash program" instrument. Whether it will continue to do so when, in a decade or two, there are enough skilled people in industry to take on some of the training functions, remains to be seen. That the training function assigned to the schools at present is highly effective in this phase of Soviet development goes without saying. But it is not the ideal state of affairs; for a high degree of specialization makes for a low degree of mobility. It trains specialists who may perform well in their narrowly defined field. But let the demand in that area decline and it becomes extremely difficult to shift them into other useful work.

The Russians, with their still almost insatiable demand for almost everything, may not have to worry about that problem—yet. Nor do they concern themselves much with the unhappiness of individuals in the wrong vocation. The late A. S. Shcherbakov, a Politburo member, was quoted by *Pravda* on January 22, 1941, as saying that many young people "mistakenly understood the right to work to mean the right to choose their own place of employment in disregard of the interests and needs of the State."

This is the philosophy that permits vast armies of workers or young school graduates to be shifted into one or several areas that happen to be in the limelight of a particular five-year plan. When the Supreme Soviet, for instance, saw the approaching need of a vast expansion of the petroleum industry, the technikums were ordered to turn out large numbers of students in the petroleum field. If the government believes that it will need a certain number of artists or ballet dancers or writers, it increases the enrollment of the 197 art technikums accordingly. If there is to be a special stress on competition in sports, the forty-three physical culture technikums get a larger allotment. Whenever the food industries move into the foreground of attention, the 111 specialized schools in that area are opened up to the required number of boys and girls.

It is not a question of sending students to technical institutes; it is a question of sending them to technikums specializing in fuel or metallurgy or power and electronics. A Soviet handbook, published in 1948, lists 3425 specialized secondary schools. The New York *Times*, in 1954, estimated that there are about 3700 technical training schools, which enroll about 1,600,000 students, and it contrasted this with about 1000 two-year technical schools in the United States with an enrollment slightly below 50,000. But this comparison, too, is extremely misleading, because it ignores the vast network of vocational schools and even of academic high schools with vocational departments in the United States, plus the many advanced on-the-job training facilities of American industry and business.

Theoretically, the curriculum of the technical high schools in Russia is based on the curriculum of the high school part of the ten-year school. Actually much of the general curriculum is sacrificed in favor of the specialized field of any one of twenty-three technical or vocational categories. Unfortunately only the complete curriculum of the mining technikum is available, but it probably provides a pretty typical yardstick. In it, the total of the regular high school subjects, including mathematics and the sciences, makes up only 39.5 per cent of the entire program (compared with 85.2 per cent in the ten-year school) while the specialized work amounts to 60.5 per cent. Even mathematics is cut down to 8.5 per cent (against 18.4 in the ten-year school), physics to 4.9 per cent (compared with 9.7 per cent) and Russian language to 6.6 per cent (compared with 16.8 per cent.)

Whatever the merits or flaws of this high degree of early and rigid specialization may be, it would not be applicable to the United States—unless it were to be combined with an equally rigid direction of labor. This would mean all labor, from the artist to the mining technician. For without such direction, the danger of obsolescence of the individual and of his productive and salable knowledge would be enormous. A relatively free economy, such as that of the United States, can operate successfully only with a labor force that can easily be converted from one kind of specialty to another. The American problem was perhaps best expressed by the president of Vassar College, Sarah Gibson Blanding, when she said that to train students in the use of a specific gas range or washing machine would render their knowledge obsolete by the time the new models were on the market, a year after graduation.

Someday the Russians may face the same problem of readjustment. Whenever their basic need for consumer goods, in addition to the heavy power and defense industry which now gets the lion's share of Soviet man power, is satisfied, they may have to cope with millions of obsolescent "specialists." That they are up against some of the weaknesses of specialization even under present conditions was driven home recently when Nikita Khrushchev complained publicly that Soviet agricultural technikums are turning out people who are afraid of cows. And *Pravda*, on September 15, 1954, said: "In some technikums, for example, the courses on the repair of farm machinery are given before the courses on farm machinery, and courses on the mechanization of animal husbandry before the courses on electrical equipment." But despite these slight rumblings of dissatisfaction, it will be a long time—at least a decade or two—before the Soviets find themselves driven into the luxury of more general education. Make no mistake about it, general education is a luxury which has no place in a society that expects to fulfill immediate quotas of highly technical production while the population has only just evolved from the real and technical illiteracy of the feudal, peasant state.

This for the time being, the Soviet school will remain highly specialized, highly selective, often able to produce well-trained and superbly skilled young people, yet generally unconcerned about the wasted talent of those who fail to make the grade. It will continue to have military and naval schools in which children, after completion of their first three years of elementary school, will be trained to be military men —and nothing else. They will continue to siphon off large numbers of young people into the schools for working youths where they will be given part-time training and education. They will even continue to experiment with their new boarding schools, which were established by the Twentieth Congress of the Communist Party in 1955 and which have just begun to be put into operation, mainly for children of widows and of parents who work.

All of this shows how risky it is to compare, in the quick manner of a popular magazine, a typical Russian and a typical American high school student. The most we can claim to know is just about what the best of the Russian schools offer to the best of the Russian pupils. So far we have seen that this is a good deal. We now must still ask: how does the Russian school—not according to official decree and propaganda handout—proceed in its teaching? And how well —or badly—does the American school come off in comparison with the Russian school. Or, to start at the other end: what can we say about the opportunities that are being offered to those millions of American teen-agers whom the boy on the *Life* magazine cover was said to represent?

6

*The High Price
of Excellence*

If it is difficult to draw a picture of the typical Russian student or the prototype of the Russian School, to attempt any generalization of the American counterpart is downright impossible. At a gathering of parents in an American city of about 200,000 population one mother complained that her daughter in seventh grade was assigned about two compositions per term. Another mother, whose children were in a school not more than ten miles away, protested that her little girl, in fourth grade, regularly wrote one composition a week. Both were right. The children of both were technically part of the same process of education, the same curriculum. Yet it would be absurd to pretend that they were offered an equal educational opportunity.

To prove the deficiency of American education a radio commentator in the spring of 1958 posted himself outside the entrance of a large city high school. Equipped with a microphone, he stopped a group of boys and asked them what they were studying. Several of them said that one of their courses was coed cooking.

The broadcast which proceeded to ridicule the low standard of the American high school set off a storm of protest across the country. Principals and school superintendents said that their schools offered no such courses. Others, who admitted to having some sections which included "practical" subjects of this nature, added that only a small proportion of their student body took part in them.

Again both were telling the truth: the broadcaster, who had nailed a specific fact in a specific school; the educators, who disclaimed any such teaching or pointed to special teaching for certain youngsters.

Or take the example of a large city high school—this one in Brooklyn, New York—which could be "accused" of permitting a group of sixteen-year-old boys to spend part of their day tending a garden and growing vegetables. Yet the same school offers some of the toughest mathematics courses, augmented by a mathematics team on which carefully selected "members" spend up to six hours a week in advanced mathematics work that is not generally required or even offered in most high schools.

You could easily find high schools in which the teaching of foreign languages is either extremely weak or required of only a minority of students. But there are also some elementary schools in which eight-year-olds learn to speak and write a foreign language fluently.

There are schools—and entire school systems—in which it is considered undemocratic to advance any student beyond the speed of learning of the mediocre mass. Yet it is easy to find instances such as that of an exceptionally gifted child in second grade in a New Haven public school who, in some subjects, is being taught on the sixth-grade level.

What then can be said about the American school in comparison with the Russian school? Who sets the standards? How high or low are those standards?

First it must be said that practically all American children go through the equivalent of at least six years of elementary school. More than 80 per cent go to high school, and according to the most recent estimates and statistics more than 55 per cent complete high school and get their diploma. The equivalent Soviet figure, as was documented in the preceding chapter, is in the neighborhood of 12 to 15 per cent. The American high school makes a determined attempt to lead or drag every student through the final target point of the high school graduation; the Soviet school arrives at its smaller ultimate number by ruthlessly dropping all stragglers and by unsentimentally channeling all those who are not considered fit for high school work into other "careers," including the labor reserve.

This selectivity is not by any means a novel Soviet idea. It is based on the traditional practice of almost every European school system, other than the Scandinavian and, more recently (since 1944), the British. It is a tradition that in most instances requires a qualifying examination after the fourth grade, or roughly at the age of ten or eleven, for admission to secondary education; which further demands another achievement examination after about six years of secondary school for admission to the final two- or three-year college preparatory stretch; and which reserves the right, at the end of every year and based on a constant battery of tests and examinations, to terminate the student's education against his will. The Russians have not only adopted this basic principle, they have added to it the "drafting" of students out of the schools and into the labor reserve. If they nevertheless insist that their selection is "democratic," they base this claim on the fact that the only requisite for further education is knowledge rather than social and economic background.

Thus it must be repeated: when the Soviets speak of mass education they mean something quite different from the American ideal. They interpret mass education to mean the education and/or training of great masses of people, but by no means with any sentimental goal of offering an equal educational opportunity to all.

The temptation is to let the comparison end right here: to place the Russian system on the side of undemocratic, dictatorial unconcern for human values and to be self-righteously satisfied that the American school, with its truly democratic ideal, has already achieved goals to which the Russians have not even the wish to aspire. This is pure self-deception. While the American school has solved the mass problem of getting the great majority of children into school, it is far from finding a satisfactory way of educating all pupils to the maximum of their ability and even of offering the brightest students a sufficiently challenging fare.

Picture first, the procedure which is typical in many

134

American high schools. At the beginning of the term the student selects a certain number of courses and maps out his own program. In the best of schools there are specific requirements in such basic areas as mathematics, English, history, etc. In other good schools the system of guidance, either through teachers or through guidance specialists, is sufficiently strong to make reasonably sure that the student's natural laziness will not lead him to "specialize" in the easiest mental menu. But in many schools the teen-ager is far too much on his own in this selection. Frequently he is offered a choice between "real" mathematics or "consumer" mathematics. Often he may be given his way in picking a commercial course, with stress on such courses as business English and typing, rather than the more demanding academic course. If he "thinks" that he is not a linguist he may get away without the study of any foreign language. Or, if he has selected one foreign language, say, in ninth grade, he may "feel like" dropping it two years later—either entirely or in exchange for another language that seems to have greater appeal. The "typical" American high school student in a "good" school is required to study five "major" subjects each term, but many high schools require only four and some even less. He goes to school shorter hours and for shorter terms than his Russian counterpart. In terms of time spent in school, the Soviet student's ten-year curriculum adds up to about 2000 days spent in school, just about equal to the number of days in an American twelve-year course of study. With a six-day week, based on thirty-three weeks of school each year, the Russian high school graduate has about 9700 classroom hours to his credit—slightly (but not appreciably) more than the American student after twelve years.

Leaving aside the purposes of education in the two countries for the moment, the statistical fact is that every boy and girl who is graduated from a ten-year school in the Soviet Union has had close to four and a half years of high school mathematics and almost six years of science. Against those figures the American performance—whatever the explanations and alibis may be—is not very good. For while there is no standard curriculum of any kind and while it is true that such outstanding schools as the Bronx High School of Science and Forest Hills High School in New York or New Trier Township High School in Illinois, to name just a few, could match the best of the Russian schools, the over-all record is not one to inspire either pride or confidence. An estimate based on 1954 figures showed that about 23 per cent of all American high schools offered neither physics nor chemistry to any of its students. (One saving postscript: these schools—most of them among the small ones which are being kept alive by die-hard local tradition in a meaningless fight against school consolidation—accounted for less than 6 per cent of senior-year enrollment.)

Of all American high school students, only one in five takes any physics whatsoever, and only two thirds take any algebra. In American high schools, only 28.5 per cent of the eleventh-grade pupils take intermediate algebra; only 13 per cent of the seniors take trigonometry and solid geometry.

While almost 73 per cent of the sophomores (tenth grade) take biology, only 32 per cent move on to chemistry the following year, and only 23.5 per cent wind up taking physics as seniors.

These basic figures should prove the important point: the American school as we know it today does not offer anything resembling fair and equal educational opportunities. There is little value in the argument that the best American schools are equal to the best schools anywhere. Perhaps they are. But are the best American students—or those who might be best if they were given a chance—exposed to those schools and what they offer? Obviously not. In an average graduating class of American high school seniors each year there are over 100,000 students (based on current enrollment figures) who have had no opportunity at all to study either physics or chemistry, not because they did not want to study those subjects, but purely and simply because they went to schools that do not offer them. Add to those the unknown total of the rest of the roughly 1,700,000 boys and girls who have *chosen* not to take those subjects. At best the over-all picture is spotty; at worst it is the story of an unforgivable, scandalous waste of talent.

Dr. Whitney Griswold, president of Yale University, offers as an admittedly extreme example of the "softness" of the American high school the record of a senior who applied for admission and whose junior and senior year consisted of the following twelve courses: two years of English; one year of American history; one year of typing; two years of speech;

two years of chorus; one year of physicial education; one year of journalism; one year of personality problems; and one year of "Marriage and the Family."

When James Bryant Conant, former president of Harvard University, recently completed a detailed study of the American high school, he recommended that the top 20 per cent of the student body should be exposed to a program consisting of four years of English, three or four years of history and related social studies; three or four years of one foreign language; four years of mathematics; three years of science. For those who, though part of the top group in intelligence, are considered less scientifically inclined, he suggested only two years of science and three years of mathematics, with the addition of three years of a second foreign language.

Lee DuBridge, president of the California Institute of Technology, replies to the frequent objection (even by educators!) that advanced mathematics is so tough that it can be mastered only by outstanding students: "The illusion that calculus is so tough that only Einsteins can take it is dangerous and false. Calculus is fundamentally simple." He advocates high school courses in analytic geometry and elementary calculus.

There is no question whatsoever that the American high school stands on the threshold of a major revolution. Much more will be said about the prospects of, and the need for, this revolution in the final chapter of this book. But for the moment it must be understood that the internal ideological struggle within the American public school is between the forces that hold it to be undemocratic to have serious differentiations between the type and quality of education offered to different pupils and the opposition, which replies that the surest way to destroy democracy is to adjust public education to the lowest common denominator of talent.

That the revolution is on its way was indicated by a Gallup poll of April 1958, which found 79 per cent of the high school principals questioned to be in agreement that the current curriculum does not demand enough of the student. Only 9 per cent believed that the schools are doing an adequate job.

In the past three or four years there has been a rash of books on the flaws in the American school system. Some have been serious and constructive, others have merely cashed in on the public apprehension and have battered a straw man. The shortcomings of the American school have been blamed on everything from John Dewey and the weakness of the teachers colleges to a lack of tax money and the Communist conspiracy. But the truth behind the lack in stamina of the American school is lack of a *belief* in the stamina of their children by the majority of American parents. A tough school —tough should not mean harsh or autocratic but rather demanding and mind-stretching—is an uncomfortable idea in the midst of a comfortable way of life. A tough school will bring with it inevitable failures. It will demand that some parents must admit that their children are less gifted than their neighbors' children.

The President's Report on Education beyond High School

said that the American public would never put up with an educated elite. The report, of course, meant that the American people do not want a privileged class nor a group of citizens who for reasons other than their native talent will be assured of the privilege of education. But the American people, if they want to make public education compatible with quality education, must be ready, not only to tolerate, but to demand the creation of educational excellence offered in each generation to the cream of its talent, regardless of its origin and background.

Theoretically the Soviet and the American schools start out with the same premise: to admit everybody to the same basic education process. But almost immediately after the beginning of the process itself, the roads part.

The Russian system—at each succeeding step—makes its decision concerning a child's future on the basis of his immediate achievement. The strong move ahead. The weak are dropped by the wayside or shifted into side furrows leading to lesser opportunities.

The American system tries to make its decision continuously according to the tested promise of a child's native talents and aptitudes. It relies heavily on the intelligence test. It lowers its standards in order not to leave the child behind.

Because the American system—at least until very recently—did not have the courage and the means to differentiate between those students with low ability and those with outstanding talents, it tended to offer a comfortable road to the great majority, leaving it to the initiative of an ambitious few to break through the fog of mediocrity.

This process was aided and abetted by the "soft" psychological approach to the human mind. It was considered harmful to exert pressures that would lead the pupil to compete with others. The new theory came to be—let the child compete only with himself. Since one of the motivating forces of all human nature is the lazy desire to be comfortable, the child tends to compete with his own abilities only until it becomes uncomfortable. In progressing at an ambling pace, he loses the excitement of progress and discovery. He is bored.

Paul Woodring, one of the leading new American educational philosophers asking for tougher intellectual content within the framework of democratic mass education, summed it up in his book, *A Fourth of a Nation*:

"It is bad educational procedure to ask an average child to compete with a genius or a moron, or even with a child who is mentally two or three years older or younger, just as it would be a mistake to ask the high school miler to run against Landy or Bannister or against a man with one leg. It by no means follows that it is a mistake to let him compete with his equals, or near equals, in the activity under consideration, nor does it harm the child to know that Landy is a better runner than he, and Einstein a better mathematician."

When the American teen-age girl (quoted in the first chapter of this book) said she did not think she would like to date

141

Ivan, the Moscow high school boy, because he would probably be dull, she threw considerable light on one of the reasons why the American school is so hesitant in demanding tough competition of the mind. She spoke for the public. She was the living apology for the pace that is being set for the American teen-ager. Listen again to Mr. Woodring:

"While academic competition has declined, there has been a steady increase of rivalry in the nonacademic activities of the schools. No football coach would think of trying to develop a team without competition. The student competes, and is urged to do so, for a place on the squad, just as he competes for a place in the orchestra, the choir, the class play, or the debate team. He competes, too, for the class presidency and for dates with the more attractive girls. It is only in academic spheres that competition is discouraged."

What creates competition? The answer is the incentive, the motivation, the carrot in front of the student's eyes. In a society that does not demand very high academic achievement, the carrot becomes ineffective. The only inducement for the American student is admission to one of the top, selective colleges. But there are hundreds of lesser colleges that will accept him without a foreign language, without advanced mathematics, without much more than a smattering in one science, without any knowledge of history other than, perhaps, the skeleton outline of American history. If he is a resident of one of a number of states in which the admission requirements to the state university are set by the politicians rather than by the educators, he will hold an automatic passport to higher education if he manages to drift through high school. The mores of the society around him encourage him to work less rather than more.

Compare this picture briefly with that confronting the Soviet student. He knows that if at any one point he fails to measure up to the requirements he is likely to be left behind. Once he has left the academic stream, the odds of returning to it, despite the correspondence courses and the schools for working youths, are slim indeed. In the Worker's Paradise the lot of the worker is far from privileged. In the Soviet society of today and, almost certainly, of the next two decades, the comforts, the privileges, the material rewards—next to those of the ruling politicians—are reserved for the educated technicians, the teachers, the scientists. To be sure, this is not because the Communists cherish the intellectual; it is because Stalin and his successors knew from the start that the future of Russia depended on the brain power of the trained new generation. If Russia was to skip a century and to catch up with the industrialized nations of the West, two phases of superhuman effort were necessary. The first was to create slave labor and to transfer vast numbers of peasants to the cities, the mines, and the factories. The second phase was to mass-produce the man power—from semiskilled to superskilled—to keep the wheels of a vast mechanized continent moving. It is quite possible that, once the industrial heights and the physical comforts of the West, especially of the United States, have been achieved, the Soviet Union will also sink back into a more comfortable pace. It is possible, but it is a long-shot chance to take; for the pace now established could easily, and without too much acceleration, lead to the expansionist step toward world domination.

Leaving such speculation aside, look at the carrot in front of the Russian student's eyes:

In his testimony before the Congressional Subcommittee on Research and Development of the Joint Committee on Atomic Energy former Senator William Benton said: "To the usual incentives of patriotism and of pride in national progress, Communist leaders have added most tangible allures to prospective scientists and engineers. They have made the life of science among the most satisfying in the Soviet Union.

"A typical Soviet professor gets 6000 rubles a month, ten times the average workman's 600-700 rubles. An outstanding Soviet engineer or research scientist can earn up to 40,000 rubles a month . . . In comparative standard of living, this would put him in the class of big-time American corporation presidents. . . ."

Or, take the first-hand account by reporter Patricia Blake in *Second-rate Brains*. After describing the stipends and the comfortable quarters of the students at Moscow University, she writes: "No wonder the Smirnovs [a married couple who are student physicists] rarely venture off the university campus on Lenin Hills overlooking Moscow with its wretchedly crowded, squalid tenements. Even the palaces and entertainments of Moscow have little attraction for them. Their university is a Soviet-style palace, a fantastic complex of 27 buildings containing enough unfunctional waste space to delight the most extravagent Czar. The Smirnovs walk to their classes up velvet-carpeted stairways, past huge mosaic murals and golden statues, through miles of marble-columned corridors and lobbies that have a comfortable smell of cabbage being cooked in the dormitory kitchens upstairs.

"As for entertainment, not even Party Chief Khrushchev, who has the old imperial box at the Bolshoi Theater always in readiness for his pleasure, is as royally entertained as the Smirnovs. Moscow's best repertory theaters, symphonic groups, and opera and ballet companies perform regulary in the tremendous university auditorium beneath glittering crystal chandeliers. While five million people must stand in interminable queues for tickets at Moscow's 51 movie houses, students can see the latest movies every night at the university. While Moscow has only a few prohibitively expensive restaurants where top bureaucrats, military men and their wives can afford to dance to a band, students can dance every Saturday night to professional orchestras in any of several university ballrooms . . ."

This is a powerful carrot. It becomes all the more powerful as long as alternative offers little more than wretchedness. These are the incentives which make Russian students rush into the toughest careers. Only thus can they escape the misery of being part of the anonymous mass.

Mme. Dubrovina casually spoke to me about "setting quotas" of engineers or teachers or research experts to be filled within a five-year plan. "But how will you know that you will get the required number of youngsters to enter those fields, to fill the places at the university?" I asked, hoping to trap her into admitting that coercion was used. "Oh, that's no problem," she replied. "We simply open up more places in the universities. We always have more applicants than we can admit."

The fact is that there is a tremendous surge of young people trying to get into the fields for which learning is required. They are the fields of privilege, of better life, of popular esteem. Those, incidentally, are also the areas in which it is easier to escape from the political pressures and the mental imprisonment of the police state. The only other way to escape the wretchedness of Soviet life is by being part of that other privileged group—the politicians, and for them the educated youth of Russia has little more than condescension, hatred, and contempt. The young student in Patricia Blake's report looked with anger on his classmates who had made their way through pull rather than hard work. "They don't bother with the sciences," he scoffed. "They . . . write snap theses on socialist-realist traditions in North Korea poetry, and five years from now, they'll be standing on platforms, talking my ears off about the need for hard work and self-sacrifice."

These are powerful incentives: the escape from oppression and the promise of material comforts. But they are not incentives that work in favor of a tougher education in the United States. This country's youth is fortunate enough not to have to escape from oppression, and there are many ways of being "a success" without too much hard work in school.

The problem then becomes one for society as a whole. It is a question whether—perhaps under the oversimplifying spur of a Sputnik—the American people can recapture a sense of urgency about intellectual preparation. Will parents learn again to be pleased when their children are made to study harder? Will they put up with the moans of their sons and daughters over tough problems and over assignments they think they cannot complete? Will communities cease to argue that they cannot raise the pay of their teachers because they would otherwise have to give equal benefits to their policemen and firemen? It is one of the great ironies of this century that a police state rather than a democracy thinks more highly of its teachers than of its policemen.

None of these questions can be answered by emergency legislation, although a certain amount of emergency thinking may be essential. Nor can they be solved by government decree. In fact, before any question can be answered, the future supply of teachers must be assured.

Mme. Dubrovina assured me that there was no shortage in Russia. The statistics bear this out:

While the United States is struggling to maintain a teacher-student ratio of one to thirty, the Soviet Union in 1956 reported a ratio of one to seventeen. The United States, with a total student enrollment on all education levels, including higher education, of about 40,000,000 has approximately 1,450,000 teachers. The Soviet Union, with a total enrollment on all levels of about 30,000,000, has 2,047,000 teachers. To teach elementary and secondary school science, United

States schools have a maximum of 160,000 teachers; the Soviet Union, 370,000 teachers. Thus the Soviet Union can boast of more than twice as many science teachers as are now employed in American schools.

None of these comparisons is absolute. The argument will go on forever whether certain numerical totals can be accepted as a guarantee of higher standards of education. In fact, a later chapter will show some of the serious flaws in the Russian teaching process. But one fact must be accepted as self-evident: a school system that is able to staff its schools with a sufficient number of teachers is at a definite advantage over a system that suffers from a serious shortage. Whether the teachers at hand are used to the best advantage, whether they are properly trained to do their job, is another question.

Finally, no comparison between the American and the Russian schools can be meaningful without some analysis of the two nations' willingness to pay for their education. Those comparisons are not easy, and they are often extremely rough. Occasionally newspaper reports—encouraged by the Soviet propaganda machine—spread alarming figures, putting the Soviet education budget as high as one third of the total national budget. This is, of course, a gross exaggeration in the light of Russia's gigantic outlay for defense and industrialization. It should also be remembered that to the Soviet statistician "education" is an all-inclusive term. When he adds the totals, he includes in them not only the schools and colleges. He adds to the figure everything from correspondence courses to propaganda, newspapers, magazines, movies, theater, radio, and television. Naturally, if the American total were to include the many private budgets, ranging from the television networks to the thousands of publications in the world of books and newspapers, the comparison would not be so alarming.

Even after these qualifications have been allowed for, the picture of Soviet spending, compared with American support of education, remains impressive. Bear in mind that the Russian gross national product—the total of useful goods produced, and thus the most realistic yardstick for national wealth—is between one fourth and one third of the American total. The United States spends between 2.6 and 3 per cent of its gross national product on education; Russia spends approximately 7.4 per cent. In higher education, the United States spends about 0.7 per cent; the Soviet Union spends about 1.5 to 2 per cent. The United States spends about 1.5 per cent of its gross national income on research and development; the Russian equivalent is estimated to be somewhere between 10 and 20 per cent.

The Soviets have a built-in, though perhaps only temporary, advantage in making academic careers attractive in comparison with the drabness of the rest of the social-economic scene. Similarly they can, at this stage of their national development, spend a greater proportion of their "education ruble" on learning itself rather than on the facilities. In a setting of general austerity, the students and the parents make relatively few demands on outlay for physical facilities. Report after report by eyewitnesses of Soviet education confirms that even some of the show-place schools are in un-attractive buildings, with bare light fixtures and few aesthetic or athletic frills. In a society of plenty, such as that of the United States, the facilities of its institutions follow, except in times of grave emergency, the level of the general standard of living.

At present the Soviets think nothing of putting their schools on triple sessions if they are short of facilities. But they do this by holding their students to Spartan hours, rather than by cutting the total requirements of the curriculum.

These are "advantages" of the relatively primitive society that the United States, accustomed to its standard of living, cannot imitate. On the contrary, there is no doubt that, as the Soviet Union catches up in the production of consumer goods, it will try hard to imitate the "softer" American life and attitude. But in the meantime, one conclusion is inevitable: a prosperous society will have to spend more, per student, to equal the educational level of the austere schools of the Soviet Union. And when, as is generally the case in the United States today, the money available to pay teachers, even in the most up-to-date, chromium-plated schools, is far from suffi-cient, then the quality of education will suffer seriously. This is even more certain to happen if the standards of social esteem are closely linked to the personal income level of the teacher in comparison with other professions. Every visitor to the Soviet Union is impressed with the respect, bordering on adulation, shown toward teachers. Those who have earned higher academic degrees are even "set apart" by a special diamond-shaped emblem worn on the lapel. Ordinary teachers who win special awards for outstanding performance are publicly honored and widely publicized.

Compare this with the status of the American teacher, judged, inevitably, by the level of his or her income. One of every four teachers in the United States receives less than $3500 a year. Approximately 46,000 earn less than $2500. This leads to a vicious circle: low pay leads to an increasing influx of low talent into teaching careers. President Lee DuBridge of California Institute of Technology, put it bluntly: "Let us face it, we have not attracted, by and large, the smartest of our young people in recent years, into the teaching profession at the elementary and high school levels. It is true that teaching has other attractions beside the monetary one. But unfortunately, the low salaries are but a symbol of the low regard in which the teacher is held by the community. The prospective teacher also soon learns that the salary he will earn depends not on how well he teaches, but only on how long he has taught. . . . This I regard as a disgraceful situation, and it has done much to attract into the profession the slow and lazy and repel the able and ambitious." Whatever else may be said about the flaws of the Soviet system, it does not open its ranks to the slow and lazy. The premium is on hard academic work.

Nor is the lack of high-quality teachers in any way offset by quantity. In 1956 the American colleges turned out only 4320 qualified science teachers, and of that pitifully small total only about 2500 actually decided to go into teaching.

Part of the reason—a powerful part—was that in the same year the average beginning salary for science teachers was $3600, while the average starting pay for engineers was $5200.

Although a few enterprising American communities have corrected these inequities in teacher salaries, there has been no serious nation-wide effort to enhance the status and training of the elementary and high school teacher. No "crash program" can provide in a hurry the teachers who should have been educated twenty years ago.

No amount of sloganeering can change the true values of society. Russia can manipulate its teaching corps with such levers as the threat of demotion to a lower rung on the Soviet social ladder or the promise of public acclaim. There is only one real lever in the United States public school system: taxpayers' money. The popular esteem for teachers will show little improvement until better salaries attract into the teaching ranks a higher caliber of intelligence. It will be a long time before Americans will forget that the lowest scores in the national draft tests were handed in by the students of the teachers colleges. There are many good teachers in the American schools today; but there is nothing approaching the mass of good teachers that a mass-education system must have if it is to succeed.

Though the American school is older than the Soviet school, they are both—in terms of history—very young experiments. Both have yet to prove their ability to survive and to insure the survival of the societies they serve.

7

Behind the Façade . .

We have compared the stated goals, the methods, and the approaches of Russian and United States education. But now let us look behind the scenes in both systems and see how they measure up in actual practice.

The very best of the college-preparatory American high schools, for example, offer 300 to 400 more classroom hours in their last four years than do the Russian ten-year schools during the same period. The mathematics offered in some few of these schools, such as the Bronx High School of Science or the Baltimore Polytechnic Institute, is of higher quality than that of the Soviet schools. It may include introductory calculus, which the Russian high school does not offer. By way of direct but rough comparison of this type of American "elite" school and the Russian ten-year school, this is how the different subject areas correspond in approximate figures:

SUBJECT	RUSSIA	U.S.
Science	1100 hrs.	6–700 hrs.
Mathematics	800 hrs.	800 hrs.
Humanities	1700 hrs.	1800 hrs.
Shop training	400 hrs.	1200 hrs.
Physical Education	300 hrs.	300 hrs.

This table, however, tells an incomplete story, for it compares the *exceptional* American school with its ordinary Russian counterpart.

Take, on the other hand, the minimum requirements for admission at a good American engineering college. The Massachusetts Institute of Technology requires the equivalent of 630 classroom hours of mathematics, including algebra, plane geometry, and trigonometry. The Soviet ten-year school provides 798 hours of mathematics, including solid geometry.

M.I.T. requires only one year of physics—about 180 hours—and no additional science. The total Soviet science teaching in high school (last four grades only) is 1064 hours and includes chemistry, physics, biology, astronomy, and psychology.

The total entrance minimum for M.I.T. in all subjects adds up to about 2880 hours of high school studies. The complete curriculum of the Russian high school during its last four years amounts to 4355 hours.

Even this is still a highly optimistic comparison, unfavorable as it already seems for the United States. Take finally the minimum requirements set for high school graduation by many states of the United States as compiled by Alexander G. Korol in his exhaustive study, *Soviet Education for Science and Technology*. It calls for only one year each of mathematics and science, leaving the majority of the remaining 2500 classroom hours open for electives, plus such minimum requirements as four years of English and at least one year of American history.

Nor is the excuse, frequently put forth by apologists for the *status quo* of the American school, that the lack in science and mathematics is made up for by work in the humanities a really valid one. For although the glare of publicity, set off by Sputnik, has thrown its light mainly on science and mathematics, the decline of the humanities in the great mass of American high schools has been equally alarming. Many American colleges must offer "remedial English" to their freshmen because the high schools have failed to provide even such fundamental instruction as the essentials of grammar or good writing. It is only in recent years that a rebellion against high school laxity has begun. In 1957, for instance, the University of Illinois notified the state's high schools that, beginning in September of 1960, it would no longer offer remedial English to its incoming freshmen.

Latin, which had long been considered one of the mainstays of a sound academic education, is now being studied by fewer than 7 per cent of American high school students. Greek has practically disappeared. Ancient history, which educators in the past thought to be essential to any real understanding of modern, including American, history and progress is now being studied by fewer than 1 per cent of America's high school population. The classics, for all intents and purposes, are no longer taught at all. There is bitter irony in the fact that the Soviets, who denounce the entire tradition of the Judeo-Christian civilization of the West, require of every high school pupil a knowledge of ancient as well as modern Western history. The United States, acknowledged leader of the Western world, permits generations to grow up in a historical vacuum. Granted that the Soviet teaching of history is geared to the ideological dictates of the Soviet State and its historical purposes and interpretation, it is hard to believe that even the slanted instruction of the Soviet school will not lead to more knowledge than the haphazard approach in the American school. If there is to be any intellectual locking of horns between the two rival civilizations, even the most perverted Soviet dragon, conscious of its historic mission as set forth by its own historians and philosophers, will be superior to the contented, ignorant cow that must eventually symbolize a generation that knows little more about the roots of democracy than the mechanical operation of a voting machine. It is highly doubtful that the full meaning of the American Revolution can ever be grasped by a student who is not familiar with the French Revolution, to say nothing about the Greece of Athens or the laws of ancient Rome and the evolution of parliamentary government in Great Britain.

Dr. DuBridge, when asked to address a science and education conference held at Yale University in spring of 1958 on the topic, "Education in the Age of Science," said that this talk should not have been assigned to a scientist but to a historian; for, he added, the age of science started not on "Sputnik Day" but in 1700 with Galileo. Similarly the struggle between freedom and slavery—the never-ending war, sometimes hot and sometimes cold, for the survival of man's liberty —can only be understood in the light of man's total history.

Or look at the teaching of foreign languages in the modern American school. It is reported that only one of four Foreign Service officers entering the State Department is able to speak *any* foreign language. At present only 15 per cent of America's high school students study any foreign language, and many of that small group take only two years—not enough to even master headlines in a foreign-language newspaper. By contrast, every Soviet ten-year student must study a foreign language for six years. In 1957 all American colleges graduated only 1525 students who were prepared to teach a foreign language, and not all of them entered the teaching profession. Since only about ten American high schools offered any Russian in 1957, it is hardly surprising that great masses of Russian books, some of them of great technical significance, gather dust, untranslated, in American archives.

So much for the American story at this point. What about the Russian school? We have seen its fixed, rigid, but nevertheless impressive curriculum. We have seen Ivan, the model Soviet teenager, on the cover of an American mass-circulation magazine. The question still remains: how much of this awe-inspiring curriculum is actually translated into classroom teaching? How well are Russian students taught? What are the flaws in a system which, could it be translated from blueprint into flawless operation, would be almost impossible to compete with?

The impression, created by the headlines of the day, has

come to be that every Soviet gas-station attendant is a potential guided missiles expert and every factory foreman a camouflaged Einstein.

There is no easy answer in any attempt to judge the Russian school as it actually functions. The standards and the requirements are high. The best of the Soviet teachers are probably as good as the best American teachers, and it is safe to assume that in Russia a great many more teachers are well-trained than in the United States today. Why? Simply because the requirements are tougher. The Russian high school teacher is expected to be a scholar in his field and not, as is frequently the case in the United States, merely a college graduate with a rudimentary knowledge of his specialty.

Marc Raeff, associate professor of history at Clark University, reported in the New York *Times Magazine* of June 22, 1958, after a visit to the U.S.S.R.: "In the United States, education departments and teachers colleges are convinced that what matters is the method of teaching, not the subject matter. Thus their attention is focussed on how to teach, not on what to teach—and too often they turn out teachers who may know the methods but are ignorant of the subjects.

"The Soviet pedagogical institutes, on the other hand, see teacher training in quite a different light. Their staffs consist of scientists and scholars actively contributing to their disciplines through research and writing. Since the schools' main function is to impart knowledge, the first duty of the teacher is to have a thorough grasp of the subject he is teaching."

The Russian teacher of history—in the tradition of the

Western European teacher—is expected to study history through the ages—from ancient through modern—and, in addition, deepen his knowledge by specializing in some one period or aspect of history. Naturally he is expected to study Russian history thoroughly, although his interpretation is dictated by the Communist line. Once he becomes a teacher he must, within a twenty-year period, complete three full advanced university courses in order to be eligible for promotion and salary increases. This is in direct contrast with the American practice. We usually ask even our "experienced" teachers to take an occasional summer course to polish their "methods of teaching" rather than to enhance their academic knowledge.

Even Soviet elementary school teachers, in their four-year teacher-training course, devote the great majority of their work to the "content" subjects, such as language and literature, mathematics, the sciences, history, etc. Out of a total of 4612 hours of classroom work, they devote only 190 hours (4.1 per cent) to pedagogy, 57 hours to psychology, 64 hours to the history of pedagogy, 36 hours to school hygiene, and 212 hours (4.6 per cent) to teaching observation and practice.

Yet the actual facts of the Soviet schools do not always jibe with the prospectus or with the story presented to foreign visitors. In 1955, Mrs. A. N. Malysheva, Deputy Minister of Education of the Soviet Federated Socialist Republic (far the largest of the sixteen republics and the one containing the district of Moscow), said bluntly: "There are more than 150,000 (about 18 per cent of the total for that republic) individuals engaged in teaching who do not possess the necessary pedagogical education. One seventh of the directors of the ten-year schools and the majority of the seven-year school directors do not have higher education." These are startling figures, and it is quite likely that these leading positions in school administration have been filled with persons of special political influence and "pull." If this is so, it will inevitably depress the standards of educational leadership.

That was documented by an almost comical complaint of a county supervisor at a Soviet education conference held in the fall of 1955. "We ask," said this educator, identified as Nikolaev, "for seventeen teachers of the French language, but they send us forty-four. We do not know what to do with all the history and the Russian language teachers for grades five through seven."

Perhaps the excessive rigidity of the Russian school, in extreme contrast to the sometimes too permissive American counterpart, is best demonstrated by this ludicrous list of twenty commandments—The Rules for Pupils—which every child in school is supposed to memorize and observe:

It is the duty of every school child:

1. To acquire knowledge persistently in order to become an educated and cultured citizen and to be of the greatest possible service to his country.

2. To study diligently, to be punctual in attendance, and not arrive late at classes.

3. To obey the instructions of the school director and the teachers without question.

4. To arrive at school with all the necessary textbooks and writing materials; to have everything ready for the lesson before the teacher arrives.

5. To come to school clean, well groomed, and neatly dressed.

6. To keep his place in the classroom clean and tidy.

7. To enter the classroom and take his place immediately after the bell rings; to enter and leave the classroom during the lesson only with the teacher's permission.

8. To sit upright during the lesson, not leaning on his elbows and not slouching; to listen attentively to the teacher's explanations and the other pupils' answers, and not to talk or let his attention stray to other things.

9. To rise when the teacher or the director enters or leaves the room.

10. To stand at attention when answering the teacher; to sit down only with the teacher's permission; to raise his hand if he wishes to answer or ask a question.

11. To take accurate notes in his assignment book of homework scheduled for the next lesson, and to show these notes to his parents; to do all the homework unaided.

12. To be respectful to the school director and teachers; when meeting them, to greet them with a polite bow; boys should also raise their hats.

13. To be polite to his elders, to behave modestly and respectfully in school, on the street, and in public places.

14. Not to use coarse expressions, not to smoke, not to gamble for money or for any other objects.

15. To protect school property; to be careful of his personal things and the belongings of his comrades.

16. To be attentive and considerate of old people, small children, the weak and sick; to give them a seat on the trolley or make way for them on the street, being helpful to them in every way.

17. To obey his parents, to help them to take care of his small brothers and sisters.

18. To maintain cleanliness and order in rooms, to keep his clothes, shoes, and bed neat and tidy.

19. To carry his student's record book with him always, to guard it carefully, never handing it over to anyone else, and to present it upon request of the teachers or the school director.

20. To cherish the honor of his school and class, and defend it as his own.

There is nothing basically wrong with these "rules." It is the memorized rigidity that sets a pattern which comes to the surface again and again. Professor Raeff reports hearing a history teacher demanding exact, slogan-like answers to his questions. When a student referred to France's Raymond Poincaré as "a bourgeois politician," he was immediately reprimanded and told that the correct answer was "reactionary bourgeois politician."

There is no discussion in class and none of the informal give-and-take of the typical American classroom. When I protested to Mme. Dubrovina that this is an essential part of the educational progress, she replied that its effect was simply to "confuse" the pupil and to "waste the time" of the teacher and the other students.

The Soviet pupil is required to do a great deal of homework, beginning with one hour in first grade and leading up to three to four hours a day in the last three high school years. But the nature of the homework is not, as might be expected, independent research and experimentation; it is largely repetition of the lessons executed in school. Originality and independence are not among the strong points of the Soviet education process. Probably as a result of the sheer volume and the uninspiring nature of the school requirements, complaints have mounted in recent years. In May of 1956, an article in *Literaturnaya Gazeta,* signed by nine important Soviet doctors, warned that the Soviet education pressure was playing havoc with the children's health. They wrote: "Chronic overexhaustion, frequent headaches, weakened memory and vision, proneness to infectious diseases with various complications result in a general weakening of the child's organism." They charged that some high school students were required to work twelve to fourteen hours a day while pupils in schools of art and music sometimes reached an incredible total of sixteen hours.

Probably one of the serious weaknesses of the Soviet system of education is its lack of stability, its constant dependence on the official dictum. For while it is true that there is no central Ministry of Education (there is such a ministry for higher education), the separate ministries for each of the sixteen republics must, in all matters of important policy, conform to the dictates of the Communist Party Congress. When a new "line" is handed down it is done without much subtlety.

Take the example of the statement of the Communist Central Committee in 1931, attacking the syllabus for the sciences: "The missing elements of statics, the concept of force, and Newton's laws must be introduced in the physics syllabus; in biology—the knowledge of cell and cell structure or organism; in chemistry the syllabus must be more systematically structured to assure the mastery of elementary concepts in chemistry."

In some fields, such as history, the complete rewriting of the syllabus is expected whenever the party line changes. The teacher merely carries out the policy determined by higher authority. I asked Mme. Dubrovina whether the teacher could stray from the beaten path of the official textbook. She said simply: "First the teacher must cover the ground demanded by the textbook. If she still has time then to use additional books, she may do so." Here again is the peculiar conflict and contradiction: on the one hand the Soviet teacher is much more truly a part of the community of scholars than his American colleague; and at the same time his authority is limited in a manner which would outrage a self-respecting American public school teacher.

These limitations on the individual judgment of the Soviet teacher are not merely political. The syllabus also lists in minute detail the topics to be covered, the class hours to be spent on each topic, and often even gives an estimate of the homework to be required. These technical requirements are underlined by the ideological ones. In 1952 the mathematics syllabus demanded that "while teaching mathematics, the teachers should realize the general goals of a Communist education—formation of a Marxist-Leninist world outlook, inculcation of Soviet patriotism and Soviet national pride, and the development of will power and character."

One of the levers by which the official line can be effectively manipulated is the textbook. Soviet educators are almost unanimous in admitting the superiority of American books. They rarely admit that the basic weakness of the Russian books is in the central control of selection and distribution. Without the competition of the American textbook publishing enterprise, it is hard to see how anything better than a routine compliance with the official line can be expected. In 1954 *Pravda* charged that while there were unquestionably enough textbooks to satisfy the needs of the school system, "facts show, however, that the textbook trade is poorly organized in many cities and villages. Millions of textbooks lie in warehouses, stores, and shops . . . when at the same time there is a shortage of them in many schools." Less than a year later, the Literary Gazette complained that children in Odessa found it impossible to buy textbooks, while "at the same time tons of textbooks are sitting in a damp warehouse at the Odessa railroad station. Many textbooks have remained there for years." (Pupils must buy their own books; but the price is low, averaging less than twenty-five cents per book.)

But even the chaotic distribution of textbooks is a minor

problem compared to the problems created by the ideological changes in Soviet policy. When the de-Stalinization got under way, for instance, the Soviet school went into an ideological tailspin. Millions of textbooks had to be rewritten. E. I. Afanasenko, Minister of Education of the Soviet Republic, said in February of 1956: "One must admit that the cult of J. V. Stalin's personality has negatively influenced the content and educational work of the school. It has widely penetrated the school syllabi, especially those in the history of the U.S.S.R., general history and literature, the textbooks—from the primers and readers for the first-graders through the textbooks of the normal schools, and also reference texts published for the schools, instructions for the teachers, and educational journals."

In short, everything! Everything, it should be added, except mathematics and science texts. Those are not only left untouched by the ideological manipulators, they are, if anything, kept untouched too long. The most frequently used algebra text, reports Alexander Korol, is a book by A. P. Kiselev, published in 1888 and practically unchanged since then.

But textbooks are, of course, only a minor aspect of any education system. Far more important is the quality of instruction and the yardsticks by which students and teachers are judged. An earlier chapter has already referred to the return to strict testing and great stress on competitive grading. While the Soviet Union does, in fact, set the kind of rigid national standards that many present critics of American education are asking for, the effects are pretty dubious.

To be sure, there is an army of inspectors who check on the teachers' performances, but in a tightly controlled police state—indeed in any bureaucracy—this kind of supervision leads to inevitable excesses of bribery and favoritism, as well as to fear, fraud, and forgery. As the examination became the tyrant of the Soviet school, feared as much by teachers as by students, a new disease swept the country. It was known as "percentomania" and its symptoms were constant percentage ratings, held as a threat over the teachers' heads, much in the same way as Trendex and other rating systems tyrannize stars, producers and program directors in the American television and radio industries.

The inevitable happened. Russian teachers, being human and being afraid of losing their jobs, protected themselves by faking the grades they gave their students. The technical term is "upgrading"; the effect was that the statistics, based on Soviet examinations, became relatively meaningless. The Soviet government and its officialdom, although actually the cause of this new numbers game, then stepped in and condemned "percentomania" as "a practice which profanes and perverts" the purposes of education. And while the government has been fighting this battle ever since the late thirties, an editorial in the Baku *Worker*, as recently as January 1955 says: "Not infrequently the work of the schools is judged in the percent-of-success basis. 'Percentomania' leads to an artificial raising of marks." It was in 1956 that Mme. Dubrovina startled teachers and principals in New York by invariably asking, no matter what the age group of the classes she visited: "How many of this group will fail?"

In spite of repeated efforts to get away from this domination by marks and percentages, the examination continues to hang heavily over the Soviet education scene. In 1944, three all-important examinations were introduced: after the fourth grade, at the age of eleven; after seventh grade, at the age of fourteen; and at the end of the ten-year school, the crucial point at which those students who have survived get their chance for higher education.

As in the days of the Czarist schools, students who finish their Maturity Certification Examination with top grades in all subjects—Russian language, literature, mathematics, physics, chemistry, history, and foreign language—receive a gold medal, which serves as an automatic admission ticket to the university, provided the field of the student's major interest is not overcrowded at that particular time. In recent years, however, the university enrollment had become so inflated that even a gold medal has tended to lose its value. Universities frequently have closed their doors to all except those few who could pass the university's own entrance examination.

Here again the results of "percentomania" made the Maturity Certificates of doubtful value. Even though all students had presumably passed the same courses and completed the same amount of work, the universities looked over their freshman class applicants of 1945 and, in words that must sound familiar to many American deans of admission, complained in an official statement issued by the Commissar of Education in December of that year:

"Many graduates of the secondary schools, especially of the schools in the rural areas, have shown poor knowledge of the Russian language and of national literature. Rubber-stamp-like phrases in the written compositions and in oral answers testify to the still insufficient attention given by the schools to the cultivation of the pupils' spoken language and to their general development.

"In the area of mathematics, the absence of sufficient skill in making rational and rapid calculations in arithmetic and algebra is typical of the secondary school graduates, as is also the weakness in three-dimensional visualizing and an insufficient development of mathematical thinking.

"The graduates know historical facts and the most important chronological dates included in the syllabi but do not always demonstrate the necessary understanding of the significance of the individual historical events.

"Freshmen entering institutions of higher education still reveal an insufficient ability to apply their knowledge in physics and chemistry for the solution of practical problems and for the explanation of the various physical and chemical processes."

The causes of these deficiencies are not hard to guess. The first, and perhaps most important, is the uninspiring character of rote learning; the second is the great amount of time spent on cramming for examinations rather than on learning for the sake of gaining knowledge and understanding. Between the beginning of the fourth and the end of the tenth year, the average Soviet pupil between 1946 and 1954 had to pass thirty-six oral and sixteen written tests. Even though the total was substantially reduced in 1954, as a result of strong pressures by educators and parents, the over-all test requirements are still forbidding.

What makes the Soviet examinations a particularly vicious creation of the totalitarian mind is the fact that the testing mania forces students and teachers to become the slave of the questions that will be asked. The procedure is simple: the questions, especially for the oral tests, are put on tickets. The complete set of tickets is distributed weeks in advance, and students are encouraged to solve the problems on all the different tickets used for each test. Naturally the temptation is to memorize formulae or even answers, rather than to learn to reason the problems through to their solutions. On the day of the test, the tickets are placed, face down, on the teacher's desk, and each student is asked to "draw" as in a lottery.

It was not until the fall of 1956 that most of these examinations with their strait-jacket effect on learning and teaching, were eliminated. The seven-year final examinations, which determined whether a student would be permitted to take the last three years of college-preparatory high school work, were reduced from eleven to three examinations: an oral and a written test in Russian and a written examination in mathematics, including both arithmetic and algebra.

The most recent relaxation in the formal requirements of

the Russian schools has reduced the examinations for the prized Maturity Certificate to the following seven subjects: a written examination in literature and oral examinations in algebra, geometry, physics, chemistry, history, and one foreign language. Furthermore, the student is tested only on the content of his senior year in high school, plus a few of the major principles learned earlier. Such tests in the past covered the student's entire ten-year period of studies.

While the ordinary promotion tests are now prepared by the individual schools, the ten-year finals are still drawn up by the Ministry of Education. The Ministry, however, publishes pamphlets containing all the examination material months ahead of the actual tests and distributes them either free or for a nominal fee. Thus, a student who, for example, makes it his business to study—or memorize—all the topics or questions of each of the thirty-one literature tickets or forty history tickets should have a pretty easy time when the examination finally comes around.

In order to graduate, a student must get at least the grade of "3" (5 is the top grade, 1 is failure) in all his subjects, plus a "5" in conduct. Since conduct includes such intangibles as a student's response to the demands of Soviet ideology, the school holds a powerful threat of failure through lack of conformity and orthodoxy over the head of every Soviet boy and girl.

No figures are available on the number of those who, on the basis of these stiff last-year requirements, fail even to qualify for the Maturity Examination. Those failures must, of course, be added to those who are permitted to take the tests but don't pass them.

Not only are the Russian test questions known months ahead of the examination date, but essentially the same questions are used year after year. Without this knowledge of the procedure, the exams seem overwhelmingly impressive. For example Korol quotes the American reporters, Joseph and Stewart Alsop, who wrote in an article in *The Saturday Evening Post* of April 28, 1956: "Judging by the last year's Soviet equivalent of a college-entrance examination in physics, Russian boys know about as much physics by the end of their last year in high school as the physics majors at the Massachusetts Institute of Technology have learned by the end of their sophomore year."

Misleading? Why? Mainly because the Russian test, as it is actually administered, does not give us a true index to the student's knowledge. The best we can say is that the Russian high school senior is able to pass a test in physics and in several other subjects with which many American high school students have not yet made any acquaintance whatsoever. To translate this into concrete figures, there were 1,200,000 Soviet high school students in 1956 who were able to pass the algebra and physics test required for the Maturity Certificate. During that same year, there were about 1,652,000 American high school graduates of whom only about 10 per cent—or about 165,000—were able to take the College Board Advanced Mathematics Examination. Granted that this test may require a somewhat higher degree of understanding and skill than the Russian equivalent, it is still likely that among the vastly greater number of qualified Soviet students there would be enough bright youngsters who could match the few Americans who had advanced to this level of math studies. As for physics, only about 2 per cent of all American high school graduates were ready to take the advanced physics test, which would be the rough equivalent of the physics test required of 100 per cent of the Soviet high school graduates.

And despite this, the picture of a Russia in which every child is offered an equal opportunity to an education far superior to that offered to most American youngsters is absurd. True, the Soviet high school graduate who does survive the rigors of the ten-year school and the erratic chances of selection along the way may be offered a wider range of studies and a better opportunity to gather knowledge in areas that are either closed to the American teen-ager or are only half-heartedly opened to him. But what about the Soviet teachers' publication, *Uchitelskaya Gazeta*, which complained in the fall of 1957: "We are always told about schools being built in rural areas, but so far we have not seen much in the way of results?" Or what about the complaint by school inspector P. Reshotkov: "In our district, we have failed to fulfill the plans for registration of children of school age or the plans for graduation from the seventh grade"? Or try to explain away the charge made in the same journal on August 1, 1957, that many language teachers in the Soviet school system fail to know the language they teach and that some of them are even deficient in Russian.

For years the American public—led by its press and its political spokesmen—has laughed away and shrugged off all thoughts that the Russians could be a serious competitor to United States know-how in anything, from industrial production to education. Then Sputnik went into orbit, and overnight the American superiority complex took a nose dive. The new national mentality is that of an equally irrational inferiority complex.

This chapter has tried to present the Soviet schools in their true dimensions, without minimizing them and their achievements, but also without inflating them to superhuman flights.

The irony of the current "cold war of the classroom," with all its attempts to "catch up" and to "imitate," is that while a Soviet high school graduate's final exams may seem to test a good deal of knowledge that is beyond the American twelfth grader, any French high school graduate would find the Russian exam a breeze. In fact, the Educational Testing Service in Princeton, after analyzing Soviet Maturity Examinations, found that they demanded less knowledge in physics and mathematics than was expected of a Norwegian high school graduate. An airmail letter to Oslo or to Paris is all any American educator needs to secure the information necessary to study those two school systems, their requirements, and the successes. It could be done without any secret studies, without the services of a Central Intelligence Agency.

And yet—all eyes are on Moscow. It appears, if the headlines and expert travelers on their guided junkets are to be believed, that the Soviets have found the key to that elusive blend of quality and quantity in a mass-education system.

We have already seen the limitations the Soviets have actually placed on the "mass" approach to their schools. We have witnessed the unsentimental channeling of students into the lower regions of the education kingdom. Now it remains for the Russians themselves to tell us how final, ultimate, and perfect they think their own system really is and what they propose to do with it in the future.

Renovating
The Red Schoolhouse

"It is high time, I think, to repattern decisively the system of schooling for our growing generation." This is not the warning issued by an American critic of United States public schools. Nor is it the reaction of an American politician to the threat of Russian missiles. Neither is it an American college dean, throwing up his hands in despair over the shoddy training of the incoming class of freshmen.

The man calling for such a drastic school reform is Nikita S. Khrushchev, the Soviet Prime Minister and Communist party boss, challenging the entire system of Russian education. When? On April 19, 1958—at the very moment when some Americans were demanding that the American schools be reshaped in the Russian image.

It would be the supreme irony of twentieth century history if the American schools were to respond to the Russian "example" at the very moment when the Soviets call for drastic reforms and fundamental changes. It is therefore of desperate importance to know what those changes are going to be. Although it is always impossible to predict accurately the new turns that any institution of Soviet power, including the schools, are about to take, the immediate outlines of the shape of things to come are emerging quite clearly. Anyone who is interested in the nature of the Russian schools ought to take a hard look at the plans that are now well beyond the blueprint stage. They are in process of being introduced, and Khrushchev's language, condemning the current education scene, is strong enough to make it probable that the changes will be brought about with all the ungentle force of previous Soviet educational revolutions.

For several years now the Soviet schools have been reducing rather than increasing the academic content and the course requirements. As pointed out in the preceding chapter simple health problems forced school authorities to lessen the students' work load. But this was only part of the reason behind the move for relaxation. As the Soviet schools have become more and more universal, the Russians have begun to run up against the same human limitations that have stymied American educators for the past several decades. It is all well and good to talk about advanced mathematics and physics for everybody. The plain truth is that not every child can *take* physics and geometry—and this applies to the "New Soviet Man" just as much as to the old-fashioned Western variety of frail humanity. At the very moment at which some of the "softer" courses are being subjected to ridicule by Americans who look admiringly to Moscow, the Soviets are beginning to offer an alternate curriculum that cuts down on mathematics and science, substituting for it such "practical" courses as are offered in the American non-college preparatory curriculum. They are, besides, toying with three "new" kinds of high schools. One—and this will raise the eyebrows of a good many Americans who have been pointing out that the Russians are not easily seduced by such "frills"—will actually be built around "home economics"; another will be called a "life program" and has just been inaugurated as an experiment in fifty schools, which are sending their students into factories for half of each school week; and the final program, still in the discussion stage, would actually follow the United States-British pattern of a three-stream high school, with some students entering the mathematical, some the scientific, and some the humanistic stream.

These reforms are not entirely inspired by pedagogic theorizing from educational leaders. Within the past two or three years, the ten-year schools have been producing more than twice as many graduates as the universities have been able to accept. This has precipitated a real social crisis. As in most other European countries, the Russian student who aims for college considers himself a "student" by profession. He is extremely reluctant to dirty his hands. It may be another joke that history is playing on the classless society of the "Dictatorship of the Proletariat." The "students" are being threatened with "demotion" to the workingman's level.

Khrushchev sounds for all the world like George Babbitt himself, deploring those newfangled airs of scholarship assumed by today's "soft" generation. More young people, he says, should be learning manual trades "instead of studying things they never use." On April 19, 1958, the date that marks the official launching of the Soviet school reform, the Premier told the Young Communist League that "too many young people are growing up without knowing anything about manual labor and without any respect for work."

In 1957, said Khrushchev, the Soviet universities could admit only 450,000 students, and as a result some 700,000 graduates of the high schools failed to gain admission to any institutions of higher learning. Many of these took factory and farm jobs "reluctantly, as if such occupations were beneath them." He charged that some families thought "this snobbish mistaken attitude toward manual labor is cultivated."

Khrushchev "suggested" that there should be more trade schools as well as schools directly attached to factories. Soviet students, he demanded, must "know how to hold a hammer and to tell the difference between a rake and a stick."

It was probably as a result of Khrushchev's outspoken attack that lesser critics suddenly started to speak up. Shortly after the master himself had thundered that there must be an end to parents with "influence" getting their sons and daughters out of work and into the universities, A. N. Shelepin, secretary of the Young Communist League, predicted that an additional 1,000,000 young boys and girls, preferably high school graduates, would be sent to the eastern and northern provinces and to Central Asia.

A little later, on June 8, 1958, a Soviet educator revealed

that the results of physics examinations held in the fall of 1957 for scholars wishing to become physics and mathematics teachers at a Moscow teacher training institute were "lamentable and conducive to alarm." These candidates, according to that report, found even simple problems beyond them and many showed "surprising helplessness" in physics.

The dramatic demand for changes in the Soviet education system, however, was not the sudden and emotional brain child of the party boss and Premier that it may have seemed to the world. The dissatisfaction has been simmering for some time. As early as December of 1956, though largely unnoticed, the Soviet Education Bulletin of the Society for Cultural Relations with the Soviet Union, published in London stated bluntly:

"The present system of public education, introduced during the period of building socialism, is no longer able to tackle the complex and weighty problems of educating the younger generation. Besides general development of the educational network, and of polytechnization, the aim is to turn out versatile young people, able to turn their hands to all kinds of productive work and take a Communist attitude towards it."

The report charged that the schools had responded "slowly and inadequately" to the decision to revert from rigidly academic to "polytechnical" or practical training.

"Insufficient time is allowed for studying the theory and practice of modern industry and agriculture," this report charges. "The syllabi for physics, chemistry, technical drawing, mathematics, biology, and geography have not been adequately adapted to the principles of polytechnization . . . and not enough has been done to train teachers in the new subjects . . ."

And then—the most serious accusation to be leveled at any institution in Soviet Russia today: "The Soviet school still suffers from the failings of the old type of school. It is still divorced from life."

Schools and teachers come under close and unfavorable scrutiny. There is little in the preparation of today's Russian teacher, this report charged, that will tell him how to teach pupils "to work independently and develop logical thought."

"Formal knowledge" warns this critique of the Russian school, "is abstract knowledge in the bad sense of the word. It cannot properly develop either memory or mind. It erects a barrier between pupil and life . . . In a lesson, the teacher usually checks homework, explains new material, checks whether the pupils have grasped it, and sets homework. The pupils have no time for independent work, and therefore the material is often absorbed mechanically."

The report lashes out at teachers who are unable to plan their lessons because they have had little or no training in the proper methods of teaching their subjects. It deplores the "serious shortcomings in psychological research" and the absence of any real attempt to study children and the development of their minds.

And finally, there is a touch of comedy for the besieged Western teacher in the report's deadpan charge of smugness:

"There is an impression that everything had gone on smoothly, no difficulties had been encountered, everything had been foreseen," and in its demand "to study the experience of other countries, both capitalist countries and those that are building socialism."

By the middle of 1957 the dissatisfaction seems to have spread even further. An article in the Soviet teacher's periodical *Uchitelskaya Gazeta* bluntly denounced "the overloaded syllabus" and said "It is high time something was done about it."

"Every year," the article complained, "more is expected of Soviet schools. Nothing else is possible . . . One of the most serious defects in the educational process is the way students are overburdened with schoolwork. Studying is hard for children, and it must not be a burden beyond their strength. Unfortunately it often is. This is why children often lose interest in their studies and cannot grasp the content of schoolwork properly."

The plea is almost pathetic. A textbook in fourth grade is offered as an example: "The youngsters shed many a tear over its pages, it was so difficult for them. It took nearly ten years to get it replaced. But the new fourth grade history does hardly anything to alleviate the children's lot. The stories are boring. Many of them are written in colorless, stereotyped language. It will be hard for the child's mind to make out what they are getting at."

Over the years, teacher self-criticism, sometimes bordering on despair, has been mounting. A teacher complained in

Uchitelskaya Gazeta, in 1957: "Do the authors . . . know anything about children, their interests and demands, their psychological and physical abilities? Where is the sense of proportion? Where is the desire to lighten the children's work to take the burden from their shoulders?"

The criticism now hurled at the Russian school by the Russians themselves seems to include every field of study. An article in *Pravda* on November 30, 1956, and signed by forty-two teachers from all over the Soviet Union charges that foreign language teachers spend "more time talking about the language than doing practical work with it." They claim that "many mistakes are made in allocating young specialists to teaching posts. Those who have specialized, particularly in French, either cannot find any use at all for their knowledge in school, or else are sent to teach German or English, which they do not know well. In many schools, too, the foreign language is taken by the teacher of a different subject, physical culture, say, or biology."

At another point in the same article the Russian teachers say: "The absence of textbooks on foreign languages for the schools for working and rural youths is intolerable . . . Very little use is being made of supplementary teaching aids such as phonograph records, film strips, television, and so on, widely used in other countries."

Nor does the recent flood of criticism by the Russians of their own schools and education system stop at the routine of classroom work. After the success of the American pianist, Van Cliburn in Moscow, New York *Times* music critic

Howard Taubman reported that Soviet critics deplored the lack of originality in Russian artists. They excel, these critics complained, in technique and method, but they are without independent creativity and tend to be very much alike. They are trained to compete, rather than encouraged to grow artistically, independently. As Professor Marc Raeff, reporting in the New York *Times Magazine* of June 22, 1958, put it: "My observations . . . indicate that Soviet schools do not really foster originality. Nor does the student find much in his environment that could stimulate his creative impulses. The way of life, the arts, the literature, the drama, all seem to lack the spark of creative imagination." He, too, quotes an unnamed Russian observer, commenting on the difference between the Russian and foreign contestants in the Tchaikovsky music festival. "The foreign musicians *play*," the Russian said. "Ours *work*."

"The majority of our musicians," comments Russian critic Z. Vartanyan in *Sovetskaya Kultura* of May 22, 1958, "turned out to resemble each other very much in their creative character. Probably that is the main reason why a group of Soviet musicians did not reach the finals (of the international Tchaikovsky competition). It is not accidental that the jury preferred to give prizes to a French pianist who is far from the technical ability of a group of Soviet musicians, and to a Japanese, who is an interesting pianist but far from perfect in style. They demonstrated their creative individuality."

And then this Russian observer cut through all the speculation and went to the heart of the matter. "The mass shortcoming of our musicians is their leveling. Many lack bright lines of character. . . . One of the main reasons lies in the fact that attention is given principally to the development of the technical side, and the problem of development of creative individuality remains out of the field of vision."

"Dream, damn it, dream!" This was the order that, according to New York *Times* correspondent Max Frankel, was given to Soviet science-fiction writers on July 8, 1958. The Union of Writers of the Russian Republic, the report said, convened an All-Russian Conference in Adventure and Fantastic Science Literature. Soviet dreams and imagination, the conference report charged, were going stale much too quickly. Here was another instance of the independent, creative thoughts of the highly skilled, expertly trained New Soviet Man running dry.

With such variety of self-analysis coming to the surface, can we predict the next changes in Soviet schools? From past experience it is safe to assume that a drastic shift is in the works, but it would be foolish to try to present a detailed prognostication. On the basis of news reports, reinforced by intelligence reports of the State Department, however, some basic changes can already be seen. Compulsory courses in industrial and agricultural arts are being introduced in all grades of the general or academic curriculum. Beyond that, the education of the Russian child and teen-ager is being made more "practical" rather than more "academic." In his bombshell speech of September 22, 1958, Khrushchev "predicted" that within three or four years most Russian youngsters would be sent to factory or farm at the age of fifteen for practical training. His slogan: "All children must prepare for useful labor and participation in the building of Communist society."

The reforms now in progress seem to stem from economic and socio-political pressures. The new stress on "polytechnical" education—a version of the "learning by doing" approach—is in part dictated by the needs of Soviet industry and agriculture. But it is also intended as an antidote to the growing estrangement between the working class and the privileged academic elite. The frequent caustic references by Khrushchev and his lieutenants to the "idle student" who shirks manual labor and tries to get influential relatives to "save" him from work in the fields or in the factories tell a vital story. Aside from the political ruling class, only scholarly work offers an escape from the faceless army of the Soviet working class. How desperately the hopeful Russian student craves this escape is documented by stories of professors who have been bribed into admitting students to the universities, and of students who pay "stand-ins" to take their places in the competitive examinations. The Soviet planners hope the "reforms" will re-establish some fraternal ties between intellectual and manual workers.

The strict separation between the "student" and the rest of the country, incidentally, is not a Russian phenomenon. This problem has plagued most European countries for many decades. The German or French student has long considered himself a "professional" as soon as he entered the college preparatory secondary school. He was set apart even in dress—the student's cap—and many of the European anti-democratic movements between World Wars I and II drew heavily on the dissatisfied, unemployed intelligentsia. Even in the United States, after World War II, some warning voices were raised against creating such a disgruntled and therefore dangerous "academic proletariat." It is supreme irony that the American system, with its lack of reverence for the student (who can therefore potentially be used in any capacity without "loss of face"), has avoided this pitfall, while the presumably "classless" society of Soviet Russia is now battling the growth of such a privileged, potentially dangerous class.

Today the Soviet high schools are graduating almost four times as many students as the universities can absorb. Equally important, the Soviets who had proudly proclaimed the theory that all boys and girls are sufficiently educable to be pushed through academic high schools, are beginning to find out that this is a fallacy. The alternatives are preselection by way of aptitude or intelligence tests, up to now spurned by Soviet educators, or an over-all lowering of standards. Significantly, Mme. Dubrovina left the United States in the reams of I.Q. and aptitude tests.

Khrushchev's 1958 tirade against "high school graduates unfit for anything except more study" and against privileged intellectuals virtually proclaimed the end of universal high school education. If his "reform" plan is translated into law, the great majority of Soviet youngsters will leave school after the seventh or eighth year. Only the very gifted, especially in the sciences, would then complete the ten-year high school.

The public boarding schools, which were opened in fall of 1956, have been hailed by Soviet educators as the most important key to polytechnic education; but while the Soviet authorities claim that 400 such schools are now in operation and that they are the ideal instrument of education, training, and indoctrination in the eyes of many Soviet planners, their realization on a mass basis can, at this time, be considered little more than a dream and a vision. At this point, the reasoning behind the establishment of the boarding schools is somewhat reminiscent of the days, in the thirties, when many American educators held that the schools ought to take over many functions of the home. "For many reasons," says N. K. Gonscharov, quoted in the December 1956 issue of the Soviet Education Bulletin of the Society for Cultural Relations with the U.S.S.R., "the family is not yet able to tackle these problems. Many parents have not enough time, knowledge, or ability. The proposed introduction and wider use of boarding school education should ensure full and many-sided development of the child's individual ability and talent. The boarding school must be seen not as supplementary to the present system but as a model for a new system involving a major transformation in the whole method of teaching and educating children." Khrushchev predicts that these schools will bring up "the leaders of a new society, individuals of great spirit and lofty ideals, wholeheartedly serving their people . . . in the vanguard of all progressive mankind."

Chapter Eight

This should be a reminder—if such a reminder is still necessary: the purpose of the Soviet school has never changed. It is the creation of the New Soviet Man. This is the only permanent and stable element in the new Russian school. As the demands that the political leaders make of the Soviet man undergo changes, the structure and the content of the schools change. The knowledge, which had been part of the European tradition and which was taken over by the best of the American schools, has a place in the Soviet curriculum only as long as it serves the immediate purposes of the State. When it was deemed wise and opportune to destroy the authority of the school and its teachers—as in the early years after the Revolution—every step, no matter how drastic, was taken to wipe out all traditions. When industrialization called for an army of technicians, the tough curriculum of the ten-year school was introduced and every principle and slogan of the permissive period was eliminated. The educators who had honestly believed in the new freedoms of the interim period were liquidated and literally disappeared.

All this should be remembered as new directions are announced, as the Russians veer away from their rigid academic requirements and move once more toward the school as "an extension of the factory" or as they point to some 300 boarding schools as the forerunners of the Soviet school of tomorrow. The only thing that can be safely predicted about Russia's school of tomorrow is that it will serve—with single mind and single purpose—the immediate and limited aims that each group of national rulers proclaims for the successive phases of the vast nation's development.

This approach defies all traditions of educational thinking. It makes a supreme virtue of limited objectives and abandons all that has been considered lasting through the ages. None of this means that such a system need be ineffective. On the contrary, it can be expected to be strikingly successful in reaching the specific objectives that the leaders declare to be the targets for each phase of Russian progress.

What this approach sacrifices is the leisurely continuity of education and culture on which Western man has built his civilization and which American educators have tried to protect against the attacks by the American brand of pragmatists. It substitutes for continuity a blind faith in the Godlike wisdom of the rulers who set the immediate targets. This leaves us with a choice between the lumbering, fumbling pursuit of the elusive promise of a civilized future and the certainty of the limited range between failure and success of a series of five-year plans.

A simple choice? But what if the target of one of the five-year plans should include all-out nuclear war? This is, after all, the question that, in the current headlines and in the public concern with the schools that launched Sputnik, has led to America's current reappraisal of its own school.

9

*The Dragon
and
the Cow*

This book has tried to avoid the generalizations of the panoramic view; it has tried equally here to avoid an obsession with details and minor flaws. The mood of the American people is understandably one of fear of the Russians and their apparently superior efforts on the one hand, and of impatience with seemingly stumbling American progress on the other. Since the American people, like the Russians, are driven by the pragmatism of a young and active nation, their reaction is direct and simple: "See what the Russians are doing! Let's do as well. Let's catch up. Let's match their effort, hour for hour."

The approach is understandable and simple. Unfortunately, I suspect the answers are not nearly so simple. The competition of the classroom and the battle of minds is infinitely more complicated than the contest for superiority in aircraft or missiles. While there is absolutely no difference between successful totalitarian and successful democratic weapons, there is a world of difference between an educated man in a free society and an educated man in a slave society.

Chapter Nine

Does this mean that we must sit idly by, assuming that, because our goals are different from those of the Russians, we need not think of any changes in our schools? Should we assume that because the Russians are able to do certain uncomfortable things by force and coercion, it is all right for us to leave them comfortably undone? And, if the answer to these questions is "no," what specifically can be done? This final chapter will look at some of the key aspects of the Russian and the American school, which have been dissected in detail in the preceding chapters, and try to provide guideposts to the future.

1
CONTROL AND MONEY

Whenever American educators wanted to have a joke at the expense of European education, they would tell the classic though phony story about the French Minister of Education. At 10:30 A.M. this stodgy official pulled out his large golden watch, which dangled from a solid chain anchored in a black vest, and proclaimed: "At this very moment, monsieur, every fifth grader in France is turning to page eighty-nine of our standard history text." The story, after the scholarly chuckles had died down, was followed by an enthusiastic eulogy of the American system of decentralization and local control.

The launching of Sputnik shot holes into American self-satisfaction. This does not mean that Americans are ready to adopt blindly the kind of centralized regimentation parodied by the French story and documented by much of the education-by-government-decree of the Soviet Union. However, serious doubts have spread across the United States whether a school system without some national standards can assure survival in a world of all-out technological competition.

The first question to be resolved, without sentimentality, is whether there must be some changes in the American way of school control and to what extent such changes should be inspired by the Russian example.

There is, of course, an immediate advantage in a system that relies on strong central control. The Russians, though they do not have a central Ministry of Education for their ten-year school, rely for central control on the Ministries of each of sixteen republics. Or so they claim. In fact, the Ministry of Education of the Soviet Federated Socialist Republic, the most important administrative unit, which includes the Moscow district, serves as a "guide" for the other fifteen republics. Local autonomy exists only on relatively minor details, usually in the selection of folklore or in the retention of local language, such as Ukrainian, etc., in the non-Russian-speaking provinces. Thus when Mme. Dubrovina, as the spokesman for the Soviet Federated Socialist Republic, termed certain views and methods "incorrect," they were "incorrect" for every school and every teacher in the Soviet Union.

By the same token, textbooks are rewritten without local

option. There is no leeway for teachers, or even principals, to select one textbook in preference over another. Curriculum changes are introduced without any choice or alternative. Educational targets and even philosophies are reversed without any chance for any of the republics, much less any school district, to go its own way.

There are few, if any, instances of really independent or spontaneous criticism by Soviet educators. Critical articles in the press, such as those cited in the preceding chapter, invariably give warning of changes that have already been decided upon by higher authority: the Supreme Soviet or the Central Committee of the Communist party. Khrushchev's tirades of mid-1958 against "useless" academic training were preceded by press and magazine criticism along the same line for years in advance. But there is no indication that policy is changed because of criticism; on the contrary, criticism is used as a public relations technique in advance of a policy to be proclaimed later. This is an effective, if cynical, way to make sure that educational policy always backs up the immediate aims of the political leaders.

In contrast to the Russian system, the American schools are in the hands of some 50,000 local school boards, wildly diverse in make-up. They vary in size of membership, the ways in which they are appointed or elected, and in the degree of actual control they exercise over the schools within their jurisdiction. They may directly interfere with the day-to-day operation of the schools or they may be nothing more than a rubber stamp for the school superintendent and his professional staff. They may represent the people of their community, if the community is sufficiently school-minded to bother to vote. They may represent the ruling politicians, if they are appointed by the regime in power or even if they are elected along party lines.

The school board president may be a devoted advocate of better education or he may consider the school board as a convenient stepping stone to a higher political office or a judgeship. School boards may fight for the best education money can buy or they may let their policy be dictated by short-term interests of local taxpayers' pressure groups. Depending on the legislative pattern and the political whims of the forty-nine states, the school boards may be on their own in determining the standards of local instruction or they may have to follow some minimum criteria established by the education department of the state government.

The diploma of a local high school may be an automatic admission ticket to the state university or it may be a meaningless piece of paper signifying nothing more than a certain number of years of school attendance.

Under this philosophy of local control, one can find such superb institutions as Newton (Massachusetts) High School, Public School 208 in Brooklyn (which offers foreign language instruction to the tiniest tots), and the courageously experimenting Fairfield (Connecticut) public schools. One can also find high schools offering no courses in physics or in foreign languages or in Latin. Such variety has been hailed as being truly democratic, because each school responds *only* to local leadership.

This "system" has been extolled for its "diversity." But is diversity, admittedly a crucial part in any system of liberty, in itself a guarantee of high quality and success? There is diversity in chaos; yet presumably we have rejected anarchy as an educational and a political ideal.

There is diversity, to be sure, in a system that has fostered islands of excellence at Boston Latin School, at Great Neck (Long Island) High School, and at New Trier (Illinois) Township, while permitting thousands of children to be taught "science" without laboratories in the state of West Virginia.

Is this extreme *laissez faire* really the mark of democracy? In economics, planlessness used to be the mark that "distinguished" the free system. But extreme economic *laissez faire* was abandoned after it led to the great depression of the 1930s. Economic planning, regulatory measures, and monetary safeguards have now become accepted as levers that insure the perpetuation of larger freedoms. They are accepted despite the fact that those very levers, if manipulated by unscrupulous men with unlimited powers, would as easily destroy liberty as they can be made to protect it.

Many observers fear that extreme *laissez faire* has already pushed American education to the brink of its own great depression. They ask for more efficent use of such levers as are already available to elevate the quality of the schools. The colleges, for instance, though their entrance requirements, already have tried to bolster slipping standards. In recent years, some twenty of them have reintroduced foreign language requirements. Many more now demand the results of such "national" tests as the examinations administered by the College Entrance Examination Board.

This is a beginning. Much more must be done. Agreement by professional educators and their training institutions can spread new ideas, set new standards, and introduce new methods. This has been shown by such important experiments as the use of teacher aides in the classroom, the application of educational television, and the rewarding of superior high school students with "early admission to college."

But such experimental progress has not only been slow; it has affected only a very small percentage of the nation's children. There are two major reasons for this halting pace: one is the fact that it takes a long time for word to get around; the other, and probably more important, reason is that the necessary money is rarely available to introduce changes and improvements. It is no accident that even the few experiments that have led to superior performance have mostly been financed by such quality-minded organizations as the Ford Foundation's Fund for the Advancement of Education and the Carnegie Corporation of New York.

These voluntary, nongovernmental, public-service efforts are peculiarly American, and they are among the great contributions made to modern society by the American philosophy of civic responsibility. They not only must be preserved; they should be extended. But in the context of "competition" with the standards set by Russia and other European school systems this is not enough.

Before the American school can really come to grips with the realities of the future, many of the old clichés will have to be abandoned. The myth that the American school is superior *because* it is locally controlled and financed (with considerable help from the state government) must be put under a microscope. Local administration and responsibility *can* be superior to control by a remote and huge bureaucracy. Even the Russians may slowly come to realize this. *Uchitelskaya Gazeta*, the Soviet teachers' magazine, said on March 14, 1957: "Experience shows that the problem (of the curriculum) is not to be solved by the forces of the Ministry of Education . . . They act too timidly and too slowly." And yet, education does not become superior simply because it is in the hands of a local school board. If reliance on 50,000 school boards denies millions of talented youngsters a sound and challenging education, then the local controls must be strengthened by the establishment of national minimum standards.

This is a point on which observers of such widely differing viewpoints as author Max Lerner and Rear Admiral H. G. Rickover, the father of the atomic submarine, are in basic agreement.

Mr. Lerner says: "The cult of localism has led many (including some who should know better) to oppose any move toward federal financing of the needed expansion of scholarships, fellowships, new buildings and laboratories, new courses and research, added teachers and better pay for teachers. I can only say that those who are unwilling to talk realistically about how to pay for better education ought to stop talking about how poor our present education is. And we who know how poor it is had better accept the only real source from which added money can come—the general treasury, located in the federal government."

As Admiral Rickover puts it: "In no other Western country are educational institutions so precariously placed financially, so dependent on local politicians, on the whim of small communities where few have ever had a higher education . . . The future looks bleak unless in some way federal assistance can be made acceptable and some sort of national standard can be established to which diploma- and degree-giving institutions must conform."

The choice is not between the two extremes of government dictation and complete local option. Minimum requirements for the American high school graduate could easily be determined, and all schools would then have to fulfill them to grant a generally accepted diploma. Between the minimum standards and the unlimited maximum there would remain a gap so wide as to assure true diversity of the American school.

This could be accomplished by the establishment of a National Board of Education Advisers, composed of able men and women with widely varied backgrounds and qualifications representing the arts, the humanities, and the sciences; the professions, industry, and labor; the nation's parents and citizens, both individually and organized. The term of service on this board would be limited, and the expiration periods would be overlapping in order to assure both continuity of purpose and a steady infusion of new ideas and new personalities. Potential members would be chosen from a panel of qualified persons, prepared by leading civic, professional, educational, business, and labor organizations. The appointments would then be made by the President of the United States and confirmed by a panel of education leaders representing all levels of schooling from elementary to university education. The Secretary of Health, Education and Welfare would be the President's permanent adviser on such appointments.

This Board of Education Advisers would avail itself of all the information that is at the beck and call of such agencies as the United States Office of Education, the Educational Testing Service, the College Entrance Examination Board, the National School Boards Association, the various scientific organizations, and the great foundations. The Board's powers would be strictly defined to exclude any interference with matters of personnel, curriculum, teaching methods, and the selection of textbooks.

Even this revolutionary new approach to the nation's education standards would only be a small step toward resolving the real crisis of a present or imminent "educational depression." What about the local school districts that cannot afford, or are unwilling, to pay for quality education? Here is another cliché of the American folklore. It is painfully evident that some local communities simply will not find the money needed for sound and modern education. All the pious talk, set off by the shock of Sputnik, has failed to reverse this trend. During the second half of the crucial year of 1957, for instance, the voters of New York State defeated 38 per cent of a total of 107 school bond requests. This was the highest percentage of rejections in recent New York State history. In midsummer of 1958, the wealthy New England community of Weston, Connecticut, defeated a sorely needed new junior high school in a referendum. Only a small fraction of the eligible voters bothered to cast their ballot. The education-minded mayor of an eastern industrial city of about 200,000 population postponed the construction of a desperately needed new high school because he said he knows he would be digging his political grave if he were to raise the tax rate even slightly during his first term in office.

Such appalling examples, taken from the "educationally enlightened" states, make the argument for increasing federal school support overwhelming. Federal funds must not be regarded as "emergency aid." They will have to be part of the long-range plan, first to shore up, then to raise the standards of American education. Almost all informed estimates, including the Rockefeller Brothers Fund's special report on education, agree that by 1970 the total outlay for education will have to be doubled. This puts the figure in the neighborhood of $30,000,000,000 annually.

Nobody believes seriously that this target can be met

through the present sources of funds, which, in the case of the elementary and secondary schools, are primarily local property taxes plus state aid. But it is exactly the property tax that runs into the most violent, well-organized opposition. The number of local "taxpayers' groups," most of them strongly opposed to school spending, has increased almost everywhere since 1955.

Federal participation—there is already some, but it must be greatly expanded—in the financing of education could be a threat to American diversity and to local administration only if it were to replace local and state financing. If it is but one element in a diversified pattern of school financing, the dangers are small. In fact, the outcry against it, alleging federal dictation, is a durable cliché of American politics.

There have already been ample instances of federal financing without federal control or interference. During the depression, the government built a great many school buildings through the Public Works Administration, handed them over to the local communities, and was never heard from again. Probably the most important step toward the expansion of educational opportunities in America in this century was the G.I. Bill of Rights, which provided higher education for millions, among them tens of thousands who would not otherwise have had the chance. The entire scheme of scholarships for veterans was financed by the government; yet America's colleges and universities, those outspoken opponents of government interference, agreed that the program was carried through without a trace of government control of their educational programs.

Federal aid to education is no cure-all. It is not, and should not be, an escape from local and state responsibility. It is just as urgent that local communities, with some assist and some prodding from the states, reform their taxing procedures. The first step would be to make available to the schools new sources of money, ranging from specific sales taxes to income taxes.

There has never been an automatic way to prevent political control and interference in the schools. Today there is plenty of it, both locally and on the state level. A telling, though unfortunately not isolated, example was the recently "railroaded" appointment of a big city school superintendent by a political majority of a local school board, without the benefit of discussion either by the public or by the minority-party members of the board. It is no secret that countless communities manage to divert their state aid for the schools into "general funds" in order to save money on other public expenditures such as roads and sewers.

The point is simply this: freedom of every kind, whether of individual rights or the local control of education, must be protected from day to day. There is no formula that will offer such protection permanently, and the guardians of freedom cannot be absentee owners. Whatever proportion of the money for schools will come from the town, from the state, or from the federal government, interference and control by the source of funds must be prevented by continued vigilance.

To shut off an important source of money because of fear of control is a sign of weakness and cowardice. It is the equivalent of failing to equip an army for fear of giving too much power to the arms manufacturer.

2
THE CURRICULUM

In the Russian school we have seen what a school system can produce if it is used with single-mindedness. The society it is made to serve is abhorrent to us. The goals that have been set for the Russian school are far too limited for the American dream. But, despite all its limitations, the Russian school shows that education has a power that Americans have not even begun to harness.

Yet to put the Russian school on a pedestal of admiration for its quality is at best childish: the American habit of being blinded by "practical" success. French schools, though slightly "behind" the Soviets in the science and mathematics requirements in terms of hours, are considerably "ahead" of the Soviets in what a student learns. In addition, the French require a knowledge of the classics and of geography that far exceeds that of the Russian schools. German schools match the Russian curriculum in content and easily top it in balance and quality. Norwegian students, and probably all Scandinavians, were shown in a test analysis by the Educational Testing Service in Princeton, New Jersey, to be ahead of the Russians in science and mathematics. Moreover, they can easily outdistance Soviet students in the social sciences and humanities.

The Russian report card, nevertheless, has made many Americans aware of the obvious: much American education is shoddy and uninspiring. What can, or should, be done?

To my mind, the first order of priority is to put into effect the recommendations made by Dr. James B. Conant as a result of his recent two-year study of the American high school. This means that all high school students would be required to take a minimum of (1) four years of English, (2) three or four years of history and related social studies, and (3) one year of science. But these would only be the basic requirements for the "average" pupil. All the academically able students—Dr. Conant estimates the total at between 15 to 20 per cent, but I believe this to be on the conservative side—would be *required*, not just *permitted*, to add the following:

If they are scientifically oriented: three or four years of a foreign language; four years of mathematics; two years more of science (making a total of three).

For those with less capacity for science: a total of two years of science; three years of mathematics; but the addition of a second foreign language.

All the able students would be required at least five "solid subjects" each year.

All those students who are not preparing for college would be given specialized training in solid, marketable skills, in addition to their basic minimum of general education. While they would not be graded on the same competitive scale with the "academic students" in their general education accomplishment, they would compete for excellence in their special vocational courses.

Dr. Conant would also:

—eliminate (by consolidation) high schools too small to offer the proper selection of courses, or, more specifically, high schools with fewer than 100 students in the graduating class;

—change from a six-period school day to one of eight periods, even if each classroom hour would have to be shortened somewhat;

—see to it that able girls get as much mathematics and science training as is provided for able boys;

—make the course of study, including the marking of the work accomplished, competitive for the able students, while practicing leniency with those who cannot achieve high standards of scholarship;

—give able students college-level work while they are still in high school, as is now being done in relatively few school systems.

Even this broad therapy for high school ills may not be quite enough. For while it will be essential to require far more basic background courses for all students, eliminating many of the present-day "elective" courses, the improved American high school will, at the same time, have to make provision for truly demanding and independent study and research.

The present organization of the American high school con-
spires to make independent work as difficult as possible.
Homework is often held to a minimum. The institution known
as "study hall" is little more than a device to put the students
in cold storage for an hour. At best they do a little routine
work. At worst they spend the time in more or less polite
horseplay. Even in laboratory work, partly because of the
shortage of sufficient numbers of able science teachers, students too often carry out experiments mechanically by following instruction books aptly nicknamed "cookbooks." And
since the average English teacher usually has an impossible
work load of pupils, the number of student compositions
gets reduced to a dangerous minimum.

To stop this trend and to give further impetus to Dr.
Conant's reform plan, I would propose the introduction of
a special adjunct or wing as part of every high school. For
lack of a better term, I would call this haven of independent
work "the learnery." It would combine all the features of the
library, the workshop, the den, the laboratory, and the studio.

There would be stacks of books. There would be collections
of records, films, and kinescopes. There would be listening
and viewing rooms. One corner would provide laboratory
tables and equipment. Another corner would provide space
and light for artists. The mechanically minded would find
workbenches. For those who want to write there would be
typewriters and desks.

The learnery would attract leading experts from many fields
—not to lecture and teach, but to consult, to discuss, to ad-

vise, and to offer criticism. The boy or girl interested in the sciences would find outstanding local doctors, chemists, or physicists near at hand, ready to talk quietly. A student with a flare for writing might discuss his problems with a best-selling novelist or with a historian from a nearby university. There would be musicians, artists, carpenters—all of them newly drawn into the renaissance of learning. And, of course, there would be the teachers, at least the most devoted among them, to carry the spark of learning from the classroom to the search for independent discovery. Perhaps most important, in the learnery students would teach each other. Naturally, attendance would be voluntary and without reward, other than the excitement of truly independent experimentation and learning.

Nor is the reform of the American high school the only requirement. Americans will have to reappraise the entire course of the child's educational career. Questions to be asked include:

Is the American youngster's elementary schooling being stretched too long?
Should the junior high school period, if it is to be retained at all, be integrated more closely with the studies of high school rather than of elementary school?
Is the American child being protected too carefully and too long from the rigors of intellectual work?

Dr. Morris Meister, former principal of the Bronx High School of Science, says: "My experience is that 99 out of 100 children are happiest when put to work at challenging tasks."

This, I suspect, is true of children of all ages. The parents of a fifth-grade pupil in a good suburban elementary school recently were seriously concerned over their son's sudden "behavior problems" in class. When they asked the teacher, she admitted that the boy generally completed his work ahead of the others and simply was bored with the proceedings. Difficult as it may be, the American school must be able to provide a constant challenge to all students and an exceptional challenge to the exceptional students.

This cannot be done without a great mass of good teachers and a sufficient sprinkling of outstanding ones. The simple facts of American economic life have turned the odds against our building up a reservoir of able teachers. The lure of nonteaching careers promising greater immediate and long-range returns has been too strong. The underpaid teacher has been deplored to the point of national deafness, but that does not erase the fact that no real improvement is likely until the nation is ready to pay its teachers more generously.

3
THE PRIORITIES

With their first obstacle, illiteracy, out of the way, the Russians' education problem today is far less complicated than ours. The goals that Russian rulers set for the Soviet people are specific and short-range. Literacy came first. Industrialization was the next step. Now each succeeding phase deals with such narrow targets as petroleum production, jet aviation, atomic power, missiles, space travel, etc. Specialized knowledge to prepare the technicians needed for the execution of each specific task, therefore, becomes the aim of education. Training, in fact, is more important than learning. Skills are at a higher premium than ideas. In fact, ideas can be a burden in a police state with clearly defined objectives.

The rub in this theory is that, even in so tightly controlled a state and so rigidly planned an economy, the educational needs of a nation are difficult to anticipate with any degree of accuracy. Particularly in an age of unprecedented scientific break-throughs, which may make obsolete such sources of power as coal, petroleum, or electricity, any attempt to predict future manpower needs is impossible. Entire professions are likely to disappear. It took decades before the lighters of gas lamps finally became extinct; it may take only a few years to replace atomic power technicians with hydrogen power specialists.

Pravda, in June 1958, complained that "droves" of young graduate technicians and engineers were being turned away from jobs for which they had been trained. There are, says the official Soviet journal, too many of them in some fields and too few in others. The remedy, the newspaper suggests, is to get the training of specialists "attuned to the needs of Soviet industry."

It would be too much to expect of the men, who consider five-year planning the answer to all progress, that they recognize such "attuning" to be difficult if not impossible. *Kom-*

somolskaya Pravda, the youth edition of the official paper, complains that graduates "assigned to jobs" arrive to find that no jobs are waiting for them. Industries, the paper says, ask for specialists but reject them when they are provided. What the editors overlook is that today's specialist may be tomorrow's drug on the market. In fact, the Communist youth journal approaches that conclusion when it muses that the rejected specialists, when "thrown on their own devices," usually wind up in jobs for which they are eminently unsuited.

If it is dangerous for Russia to make education the slave of this kind of narrow planning, it would be fatal for the United States. Even in purely technical terms, America's industrial strength has been in the flexibility and the versatility of the labor force. President Roosevelt suddenly, on the day after Pearl Harbor, asked that the country's factories produce 60,000 modern planes. The seemingly impossible order was carried out—not because American schools had trained a vast reservoir of men and women specifically prepared for this job, but rather because men and women with basic skills and flexible minds were able to adapt themselves to the specific needs of the moment.

If America is to continue as a free nation and as the symbol of freedom, it would be fatal to rely on an education that promises nothing more than the fulfillment of immediate and narrow quotas. The Russians can afford to be "practical" about the youth they educate: they must have the skills to bolster Russia's physical power and to raise her standard of living. The American schools must accomplish a much more complicated mission. They must educate a nation of voters. They must give us economists—not just economic technicians capable of manipulating the official economic theory. They must give us historians, artists, philosophers, and scientists capable of work in all fields, from nylon hose to intercontinental ballistic missiles. They must, in short, provide the brain power of a society that is committed to do many things, even at the risk of being wasteful. They must serve a society that can afford the devoted stargazer as well as the devoted nuclear scientist.

This is why it is so desperately important to prevent the United States from being stampeded into the kind of false priorities that characterize the Russian schools. The immediate popular reaction to Russian scientific progress was a demand for a "crash program" in science and mathematics. But this reaction is based on a false understanding of the purposes of education. It assumes that there is a short-range relationship between the curriculum and technological supremacy. It takes at least twenty years before the results of a "new" curriculum may influence a nation's technology.

During World War II the United States built the first atomic bomb and thereby opened a new chapter of history. Were the American schools any better in 1940 than in 1950? If anything, they were slightly worse. Technological feats such as the harnessing of atomic power by the United States in the 1940s and the Soviet sprint into outer space of the 1950s were the result of the single-minded concentration of great and powerful nations on a specific project. Like the men and women who pushed the power of the United States to the Western frontiers, the Russians who pushed the Soviet frontier toward the moon did not rely on the excellence of their schools for these achievements. Most of the men and women who worked on Sputnik never attended the kind of Russian school that is now so widely hailed as superior. They were the product of the worst period of disintegration in Russian education. The older scientists and engineers were trained in Czarist schools of Imperial Russia, still solidly within the old German and French traditions.

Does this mean that it matters little what kind of public schools a nation offers to its youth? If technological success is the only yardstick, the answer is probably "yes." Able technicians can be trained without "education." The superior craftsmen of the Middle Ages were almost entirely the product of apprenticeship, and they had skills far superior to those provided in today's vocational schools. The American Telephone and Telegraph Company can turn out better electronics technicians than most Soviet technikums. Expert dancers, actors, musicians can be developed outside the basic educational system.

Thus, when American educators insisted on the importance of general education, they were on the right track. The mistake came in the interpretation of the term "general." Scattered and generalized knowledge was permitted to replace disciplined and specific learning. The "anything goes" theory replaced mathematics courses with courses *about* mathematics. Instead of requiring the mastery of a science, students were offered science survey courses that skimmed the surface without ever trying to dive into the depth of understanding. Mastery of art and music gave way to the *appreciation* of art and music. The rude awakening came much later: appreciation without knowledge is a shallow sham.

The folly was compounded when many educators would not even consider mathematics and science as an integral part of a general education. They persisted in classifying those subjects as part of the specialized education which they opposed.

If the American school is to return to a balanced diet and to re-enter the competition for excellence, then the general education plan of the future must resist the science and mathematics "crash programs" that are now so urgently demanded. It must instead make the sciences and mathematics an integral part of the entire education plan. Dr. Isidor I. Rabi, Nobel Prize physicist and chairman of President Eisenhower's Science Advisory Committee, put it quite simply: "We must teach science as an intellectual pursuit rather than as a body of tricks . . . As yet, if a man has no feeling for art, he is considered narrow-minded, but if he has no feeling for science, he is considered quite normal. This is a fundamental weakness of our whole civilization. Right now it's the thing which may bring its destruction."

Crash programs can be vastly successful, as the Manhattan Project, which produced the first atom bomb, has shown. In the field of defense production, crash programs are essential. But crash programs are cash programs: their major ingredient is money, a great concentration of money on a limited objective. Many of those who raise their voices in demand of an educational "crash program" today believe that this is an inexpensive substitute for costly arms expenditures. They are wrong. The improvement of the schools is a slow, long-range task. It is a matter of balance and quality, supported by a *continuing* flow of money.

4
DANGER OF EXTREMES

"There are at the present time two great nations in the world, which started from different points but seem to tend toward the same end. I allude to the Russians and the Americans. Both of them have grown up unnoticed; and whilst the attention of mankind was directed elsewhere, they have suddenly placed themselves in the front ranks among the nations, and the world learned of their existence and their greatness at almost the same time. . . . Their starting-points are different, and their courses are not the same; yet each of them seems marked out by the will of Heaven to sway the destinies of half the globe."

So wrote Alexis de Tocqueville in 1835. His prophecy has come true; it is the central fact of the twentieth century. But de Tocqueville might have added one other great similarity of the two nations: their obsession with extremes.

In building a strong and lasting education system, the

United States, instead of letting itself be thrown even more seriously off balance by the Russian "example," must shake off this obsession. While American extremism has never been as total as that of the Russians when they declared certain practices and theories to be "incorrect," the effect has often been almost as sweeping.

Take the matter of testing. The Russians have abandoned aptitude and intelligence testing completely. It is almost thirty years since a Russian student has been tested for anything but actual achievement: the lesson learned, the fact repeated, the prescribed experiment carried out. The stragglers are left by the wayside. Soviet educators justified their "uniform curriculum and uniform standards" with a "theory." In 1953 a Ministry of Education statement proclaimed in Moscow: "It is possible for all pupils to complete the work, and that is the art of teaching, to arouse the pupil's interest; that is the teacher's job." This, far from being a theory based on either scientific or biological fact, is almost as misleading as the literal interpretation of the "self-evident truth" that "all men are created equal."

Unfortunately, in the matter of testing, American schools often subscribe to the opposite extreme. They pretest a child by means of intelligence and aptitude tests and then fit him neatly into his niche. This means that the child's scope and potential is all staked out before the actual educational journey begins. The teacher can then point to a pupil's low I.Q. score as an alibi that justifies shoddy effort. Didn't the test say that there was little use to aim any higher? Thus the responsibility of attempting to stretch a child's capacity has often been abandoned.

I watched the progress of a group of elementary school children at the corrective institution of Children's Village at Dobbs Ferry, New York. Each of them had been "given up" by the public schools. Their test scores classified them as "nonreaders." So—why try to teach them? But a devoted teacher at Children's Village ignored the test scores. She fanned their enthusiasm and made them want to read. When I visited their classroom, a year after they had been "given up" by the public schools, all of them read, and they showed off their new skill with pride.

The Russian extreme has tried to force every child into the same mold, without allowing for, or responding to, individual differences. The American extreme looks at the test score and responds to the human differences—but only on a chart and without giving the power of good teaching a full and fair chance. The answer to the mass education system that combines quantity with quality is on a middle ground between those extremes. It will have to use the tests as a guide and as an aid in "sorting out" children according to their potential: not to disregard those of lesser academic talent, but to offer them the kind of educational assistance they need.

The Russian schools, as earlier chapters documented in detail, require the same, often ridiculously concentrated, fare of even the toughest subjects—science, mathematics, foreign languages—of all children. As was to be expected, the "casualty rate" was high and the percentage of those who, with cramming and superior effort, managed to pass but did not really understand what they had learned is likely to be high, too.

The American school goes to the opposite extreme. It frequently permits teen-agers to "select" their own courses, to drop subjects because they seem too hard, to omit whole areas of vital study because they are not considered suitable to the particular child's "tested" talents.

The Russian school made "failure" the threat that would make students struggle toward success.

The American school eliminated failure by promising everybody an automatic pass and an automatic diploma at the end of a given number of years in school. It did this on the theory that the psychological damage to young minds through the stigma of failure is more serious than the lack of incentive to compete for success.

Today both the Russian and the American schools are finding out that their extremism won't work. The Russians have already begun to lower their standards. They are beginning to experiment with different "streams" of education for different aptitudes among their pupils. They are even rumored to be reconsidering the use of intelligence tests. They have substantially decreased the number of achievement tests. They are, if Khrushchev's "reforms" are adopted, ready to give up universal high school education entirely.

The American schools, on the other hand, are beginning to admit that the "elective system," which gives immature youngsters a choice of what to learn, is far from satisfactory. In New York City, one of the key school systems of the nation, 1958 was the year that saw the end of "automatic promotion": more than 20,000 youngsters were kept back in their grade because they had failed to complete the required work.

It would be tragic if the next manifestation of American educational extremism were to pile more science and mathematics courses into an already chaotic study plan. One vital lesson to be learned from an examination of Russian education is its concept of continuity. Based on the European tradition of learning, the Russian school leads the student along an orderly path of studies. History, for instance, follows the natural course, from the ancients to modern times. The same foreign language is studied year after year until mastery is achieved. Biology precedes chemistry and physics. A thorough study of Russian grammar comes before the more ambitious attempts to understand and enjoy literature.

In contrast, the American school permits too much picking and choosing. It is not unusual for a student to dabble in one language for a year and then to abandon it for another one, on nothing more than a hunch and a whim. Many American students try their hand at modern European history without any previous knowledge of ancient and medieval history. Some American students dive into American history in total ignorance of the European background that sets the scene for the colonial American period. Geography, where it is not completely omitted, is rarely presented as an essential road map to history. In many schools "current events" courses deal with the complicated problems of current diplomacy and power conflicts without any background knowledge of either history and geography.

In this type of educational potpourri nothing falls into place. The student leaves high school either without feeling that he has wrapped up even a small parcel of knowledge or, worse, complacent with his smattering. He may know a little about some periods of history; but he lacks the overview of the panorama of humanity. He may have done some reading in English and American literature; but he does not really know how the currents flow. He may have taken courses in mathematics and, if he is fortunate, some science, but he does not know how these intimately related areas mesh into that meaningful fabric out of which so much exciting discovery has been cut.

Where the Russian system has forced the same priorities on all youngsters, the American system has failed to evolve any real priorities. Aimlessness was put on a pedestal and labeled individualism. This is blatant nonsense. There must be a common ground of real knowledge among a great majority of youngsters today if there is to be any meaningful bond among the citizens of the United States tomorrow and between them and the other nations of Western civilization.

5
GUTS AND SURVIVAL

The American school cannot ignore the issue of survival. We may disagree with both the means and the ends of the Russian schools. We may be totally opposed to the society the Soviets are building with the help of their schools. Yet we cannot close our eyes to the competition in which we are involved. The only escape from that competition is by way of surrender or defeat.

This means simply that the American schools cannot ignore their part in the free world's struggle for survival. In a relatively noncompetitive world, the leisurely pace of learning, adjusted to the pursuit of happiness, might have been acceptable. The law of averages and the self-propelling ambitions of an occasional genius might have sufficed to preserve American comforts.

But the world we face is competitive. As long as we are in a race with Russia, it makes little sense to say that, even though the Soviets may outrun us, our pace is healthier. There is little health in defeat, and the vanquished have no comforts.

We must do better than they in order to survive their menace, but we must do better on our own terms. To "overtake" them on their own terms would require surrender to their way of life.

What the American schools can least afford is the irrational optimism that refused to believe a police state was capable

229

of superior intellectual effort and achievement. It would be the prelude to suicide to say: freedom will triumph automatically.

The demands made by the struggle for survival are basic: to provide the nation with a well-stocked pool of skilled and trained manpower; to outmatch any technical, economic, and industrial progress achieved by the skilled and trained brains of the Soviet Union and/or any other potentially hostile power; to give the nation's young generation the intellectual and moral stamina to face the violent attacks on this embattled civilization.

At the same time, the American school system must keep the American dream alive, and this is a burden that American education must bear, quite aside from the purely intellectual challenge. In 1839 a member of a Massachusetts citizens committee for the improvement of the public schools—his name is lost to history—said: "I want to see the children of the rich and the poor sit down side by side on equal terms . . . a great brotherhood—deeming no one distinguished above the rest but the best scholar and the best boy . . ." This must remain the target.

Before the American school can meet "the Soviet challenge," it must meet the more fundamental challenge of adjusting its own sights. The levers and the incentives or threats which Soviet Russia is able to use to manipulate its learners and teachers will never, let us hope, be duplicated in the United States.

It is the drabness and the insecurity of Russian life that

glamorize the privileges of the scholar, the teacher, and the technician. The American teen-ager who fails to live up to the requirements of high school does not face banishment into the Labor Reserve. Even as an academic failure he is assured greater physical comforts than most Soviet gold-medal winners. These are the facts of comparative society—ours and the Russians'. Preaching about the rewards of hard work will be wasted as long as the rewards of indifferent work are pretty attractive. It would be hard to expect people to respond to even the most impassioned call for intellectual effort when the most leisurely pace in school assures employment, security, comfort, and, with a modicum of effort, admission to a pleasant college campus.

It is probably significant that American educators between the end of World War II and the fall of 1957 spoke eloquently and often about the schools' responsibility to teach the constructive use of leisure time. A society that can afford to worry about such pleasant prospects will not drive itself into uncomfortable exertions. The search for comfort, however, is not the best companion to the search for quality.

Educators, who should have been the spokesmen for excellence, often took the easy road: they listened to public demand. They consulted the public-opinion polls. Recently, when a school superintendent was asked whether Russian would be offered in the future as one of the school system's foreign languages, he replied: "If there is enough public demand for it, we will teach it."

There is no doubt at all that for each inexcusable folly

that has crept into the curriculum of some American schools, from co-educational cooking to "personality development and grooming," there has been some public demand. The administrators had their ears to the ground and responded. The term itself—"administrators" rather than "leaders"—tells a story. An administrator just keeps the mechanism running smoothly; an educational leader deals with ideas and knowledge. The deputy superintendent of education in Florida was recently quoted: "The training of our youth in sound practices in the operation of motor vehicles, for instance, is as important as learning to read." This is the ultimate victory of the administrator over the educator in a society grown so comfortable that a smooth ride is more important than a good book.

It is this placid, comfortable security that permits smiling, self-satisfied teen-agers to proclaim their education superior to that of their Russian contemporaries because it teaches them to get along with others. It is from this repose of comfort that an American high school girl could turn down Ivan, the Moscow teen-ager, as a dull date because he has spent so much of his time on serious study. It is this comfortable pursuit of happiness and leisure that made a group of teachers in a fashionable suburb warn an enthusiastic new colleague not to assign weekly compositions in order not to spoil the pleasant pace for them. It is in this utopia that homework is often considered an unfair labor practice.

In such a leisurely society the schools can pretend that they will get by with teachers who have had less training in their subject than have most European high school students—the Russians included. At an education conference held at Bowling Green, Ohio, in the summer of 1958, the dean of an American college "demanded" that a chemistry teacher should have at least thirty-two hours of study in that subject. A Russian high school graduate has had more than 340 hours of chemistry instruction before he gets his diploma. A school superintendent from Texas "boasted" during a science-education conference at Yale University in the spring of 1958 that his school district, in response to Sputnik, had introduced *one year* of compulsory mathematics for high school students.

At its best, the American school has already achieved great triumphs, both by aiming at peaks of true excellence and by holding fast to the principle of universality. With almost 40,000,000 youngsters going to school, there can be no doubt about the quantitative success of the great experiment. But a combination of self-satisfied citizenry and of uncertain, often downright cowardly, educators has permitted important segments of the American public schools to slip from the peaks and vanish into a fog of mediocrity.

A succinct analysis of this sorry state of affairs, comes from Dr. George Z. F. Bereday, associate professor of education at Teachers College who, after a recent visit to Russia and an inspection of the Soviet schools, said:

"The spirit the Russians have has galvanized them. They're young and they're working hard. Here no one is excited any more. We have all this—and we are going to throw it away because we won't work. Nobody seems to want to work any more. Don't change the system in America. Change the people. We must select and educate teachers better. I see our reforms as a Holy War rather than a mere juggling of courses. Here the system is perfect. The setup is ideal. But the guts are gone.

"Let's get the guts back."

Whatever the Russian schools lack, they have guts. The American schools will get their guts back no sooner and no later than the men and women who run them, who pay for them, and who determine their course will find their guts again.

In Portland, Oregon, a school superintendent found his guts again when, in the summer of 1958, he put an end to the interruptions of classroom work that had traditionally been sanctioned in preparation for a "three-ring circus" known as Princess of the Rose Festival. To his surprise, he found that parents, far from rising in protest, thanked him. In New Canaan, Connecticut, a parents committee submitted an outline that called for greater intellectual effort, more homework, and better pay for local teachers. In Levittown, New York, a group of professional men—doctors, scientists, psychologists—have formed a volunteer evening school for elementary school teachers who want to advance their knowledge in science. In some sixteen towns and cities, qualified citizens are now working as "readers" of high school compositions so that harassed teachers can increase the number of writing assignments. Several outstanding high schools have recently persuaded nearby colleges to help talented juniors and seniors with extracurricular work of college caliber as a bonus. Other schools have introduced voluntary summer courses that offer advanced studies to exceptional students.

This may be the beginning of a tide. Whether it will grow strong enough soon enough will depend in almost equal measure on the courage of the school leaders and the vigilance of such groups as the citizens committees, the Parent-Teacher Associations, and the school boards. During the past decade many of these groups have found their voice. The time has come for the test: will they speak up for effort and excellence?

History plays strange tricks. The United States was built by men and women whose traditions were deeply rooted in the European past of scholarship and learning. In America they proclaimed the unheard-of ideal: equal educational opportunity for all children. It was a revolution intended to open the doors of intellectual excellence to all who cared to enter.

Through the years "excellence" became the forgotten word, while the "open door" was made the permanent symbol. In time, despite the "open door," many children were no longer offered true equality of opportunity, because behind the "open doors" the shelves were often bare. Some of the spokesmen for education began to hint that "excellence" was undemocratic discrimination. It is the irony of history that it took the Russians to remind us, not only that excellence is an indispensible ingredient for survival, but that lazy democracy is dying democracy.

Chapter Nine

The question that remains, and cannot be answered by any book, is whether the Soviet threat will turn the United States, its people, and their leaders back toward their own strength, aims, and purposes so that they may rebuild, on their own terms and with their own brains, sweat, and genius, the edifice they have allowed to crumble.

Selected Bibliography

Adler, Irving. *What We Want of Our Schools*, John Day Co., New York, 1957

Atkins, Nickolas. "I Went to a Russian School," *This Week*, April 6, 1958

Benton, William. *This is the Challenge*, Associated College Presses, New York, 1958

—Reply to request for written testimony on nine questions put to him by the Preparedness Subcommittee of the Senate Armed Forces Committee.

—"The Soviet Tekhnikum: Ominous Threat To The West," *Coronet*, December 1956

—"The Voice of the Kremlin," reprinted from the 1956 Britannica Book of the Year, by Encyclopaedia Britannica, Inc.

—Testimony to Subcommittee on Research & Development, Joint Committee on Atomic Energy, Washington, May 1, 1956

Bereday, George Z. F. and Volpicelli, Luigi. *Public Education in America*, Harper & Bros., New York, 1958

Berman, Harold J. "The Right to Knowledge in the Soviet Union," *Columbia Law Review*, Vol. 54, No. 5, May 1954

—"The Devil and Soviet Russia," *The American Scholar*, Spring 1958

Bockris, J. O'M. "A Scientist's Impressions of Russian Research," *The Reporter*, February 20, 1958

Business Week. "The Real Trouble With American Education," April 19, 1958

Chapman, Ralph. "Rickover Assails U.S. Education Lag," New York *Herald Tribune*, April 20, 1958

Coffin, Tris. "The Crisis in U.S. Education and Why It Will Continue," *The New Leader*, June 16, 1958

Conant, James B. "The Public High School and the National Interest," Speech to National Assn. of Secondary School Principals, Indianapolis, February 17, 1958

Bibliography

—"The Superintendent as Educational Statesman," Speech to American Assn. of School Administrators, February 25, 1958

Counts, George S. *The Challenge of Soviet Education*, New York, Mc-Graw-Hill Book Co., Inc., 1957

Currivan, Gene. "Critical Reassessment Is Now Having Its Effect on the Whole American System," New York *Times*, April 27, 1958

Cutler, B. J. "A Switch: Red School System Bad," New York *Herald Tribune*, April 20, 1958

De Witt, Nicholas. *Soviet Professional Manpower*, National Science Foundation, Washington, D.C., 1955

—"Soviet Education and Its Challenge," *Mathematics Teacher*, February 1958

Dudinstev, V. "In the Staff Room," *Soviet Education Bulletin*, Society for Cultural Relations with the U.S.S.R., London, December 1956

Educational Testing Service. "The United States and the Soviet Union," Some Comparative Statistics on Education, Economics, and Social Welfare for the Period 1930–1958, Princeton, 1958

Eurich, Alvin C. "Russia's New Schooling," *Atlantic Monthly*, April 1958

Ewell, Raymond. "Education and Research in Soviet Russia," *Chemical and Engineering News*, April 14, 1958

Ferrer, Terry. "Graduation Time Should Not Mean End of Education," New York *Herald Tribune*, July 8, 1958

—"Bronx School Trains Future Scientists," *Ibid.*, May 4, 1958

—"Conant Report: What's Wrong With High Schools?" *Ibid.*, April 20, 1958

—"Month in Soviet Schools Sobers U.S. Educators," *Ibid.*, June 22, 1958

—"Parent, Principals' Views Wide Apart," *Ibid.*, April 11, 1958

—"Voters Rejecting More and More School Bonds," *Ibid.*, June 15, 1958

Fischer, George. "Soviet and American Education: Mistaken Envy," *The Progressive*, March 1958

Frankel, Max. "School Reforms Urged on Soviet," New York *Times*, July 6, 1958

—"Khrushchev Bids Schools Reform," *Ibid.*, April 20, 1958

—"Science Fiction Lag in Soviet Deplored," *Ibid.*, July 9, 1958

Bibliography

—"Youth is Scolded by Soviet Leader," *Ibid.*, April 17, 1958

—"Khrushchev Bids Schools Prepare Pupils for Labor," *Ibid.*, September 22, 1958.

Freeman, Ira Henry. "Rickover Scores School Equality," New York *Times*, April 20, 1958

Giles, C. G. T. "Why Soviet Teachers Are Opposed To Intelligence Testing, *Anglo Soviet Journal*, London, Spring 1953

Keats, John. *Schools Without Scholars*, Houghton Mifflin Co., Boston, 1958

Kline, George L. "Russia 5 Years After Stalin—Education," *The New Leader*, June 16, 1958

Korol, Alexander G. *Soviet Education for Science and Technology*, published jointly by The Technology Press of Massachusetts Institute of Technology and John Wiley & Sons, Inc., New York, 1957

Korolev, F. "Education in the U.S.S.R.," *Soviet News*, Booklet No. 24, London

Lansner, Kermit, ed. *Second-Rate Brains*, Doubleday & Co., Inc., New York, 1958

Latimer, John F. *What's Happened to Our High Schools?* Public Affairs Press, Washington, D.C., 1958

Life Magazine. "Crisis in Education," March 24, 1958

Lowman, Eleanor S. "Soviet Secondary Education—Designed to Achieve Future Scientific Supremacy," *Higher Education*, December 1955

—"Measures Utilized in the U.S.S.R. to Motivate Youth Into Science-Technology Fields," The Bulletin of the National Assn. of Secondary School Principals, Vol. 41, No. 230, September 1957

—"Washington's School for Young Soviets," *The Saturday Evening Post*, May 26, 1958

MacAndrew, Andrew R. "Are Soviet Schools Better Than Ours?" *The Reporter*, February 20, 1958

Moehlman, Arthur Henry and Roucek, Joseph S. *Comparative Education*, New York, Dryden Press, 1951 (revised 1957)

National Education Assn. of the United States. "Public Opinion Polls on American Education," Washington, D.C., 1958

Newsweek. "Down to Brass Tacks About Hours of School-Work . . .

Bibliography

What Russia's and Europe's Students Do—and How," July 16, 1958

New York *Times*. "Language Urged For All U.S. Pupils" (Washington dispatch, unsigned), July 22, 1958

—"Moscow Outlines School Reforms," (Reuters), May 19, 1958

Raeff, Marc. "Report on Russia's Big Red Schoolhouse," New York *Times Magazine*, June 22, 1958

Rockefeller Brothers Fund. The Pursuit of Excellence: Education and the Future of America. Special Studies Project Report V., Doubleday & Co., Inc., 1958

Rogger, Hans. "Frustration and Boredom in Russian Youth," *The Reporter*, February 20, 1958

Salisbury, Harrison E. "Soviet Problems Cited by Students," New York *Times*, July 10, 1958

School Management. "U.S. Schools Outproducing Russia's," June 1958

Schwartz, Harry. "Lead By Russians in Science Denied," New York *Times*, June 18, 1958

Simmonds, C. E. "Technical Education in the U.S.S.R.," published by the Society for Cultural Relations with the U.S.S.R. in London, 1957

Lady Simon of Sythenshawe. "Problems of Soviet Education Today," *Soviet Education Bulletin*, Society for Cultural Relations with the U.S.S.R., London, July 1955

Soviet Education Bulletin. "The Overloaded Syllabus," Education Section of the Society for Cultural Relations with the U.S.S.R., London, August 1957

Suydam, Harriet C. "Soviet Education Is Fine—for Reds," New York *Herald Tribune*, June 8, 1958

Taubman, Howard. "Soviet Assesses Cliburn Victory," New York *Times*, May 23, 1958

U. S. Dept. of Health, Education, and Welfare. *Education in the U.S.S.R.*, Bulletin 1957, No. 14, U. S. Government Printing Office.

U. S. Dept. of State. "Recent Trends in Soviet Schools," Intelligence Report, September 10, 1954

—"Reform and Experimentation in Soviet Schools," Intelligence Report, Bureau of Intelligence and Research, No. 7719, May 13, 1958

Woodring, Paul. *A Fourth of a Nation*, McGraw-Hill Book Co., New York, 1957